'This book is a fantastic resource, full of wisdom, compassion, and extremely practical tools for helping teenagers thrive in the face of life's challenges. It is not only essential reading for teenagers, but also for parents, teachers, and any therapists or counselors who work with this age group."

—Russ Harris, author of *The Happiness Trap* and *The Reality Slap*

"In *Get Out of Your Mind and Into Your Life for Teens*, Joseph V. Ciarrochi, Louise Hayes, and Ann Bailey provide teenagers with access to the powerful principles of acceptance and commitment therapy. The lessons are broadly applicable to any number of struggles a teen might have. Teens can't help but recognize their own struggles in the stories told and dare to pursue their own hopes in the exercises offered. Perhaps most importantly, in the midst of a stage when many peoples' thoughts and feelings isolate them from the lives they care about, these authors communicate clearly that the readers are not alone and don't have to struggle. I believe this book will be an invaluable resource for any therapist, parent, family member, or friend who wants to help a teen they care about."

—Emily K. Sandoz, PhD, assistant professor of psychology at the University of Louisiana at Lafayette

"It's hard being a human, and it's not easier being a teenager. Ciarrochi, Hayes, and Bailey clearly know what they're talking about from their own experiences and from working with youths who struggle. This is a book that should have been written long ago. I wish someone had given it to me when I was a teenager."

—Rikard K. Wicksell, PhD, licensed clinical psychologist and a clinical researcher at Karolinska University Hospital and the Karolinska Institutet in Stockholm, Sweden

"An extraordinary resource for teens and adolescents who are struggling with everything from the trials of being a teenager to more serious problems. The authors provide an engaging, compassionate, and understandable road map with practical suggestions and exercises that any teen will want to explore. It is an amazing gift to have such a useful book to recommend to teens and their families."

—Jennifer Gregg, PhD, associate professor at San Jose State University and coauthor of *The Diabetes Lifestyle Book*

"*Get Out Of Your Mind and Into Your Life for Teens* is an extraordinary guide for teenagers pursuing extraordinary lives. Ciarrochi, Hayes, and Bailey offer practical exercises and introduce us to characters who use 'bold warrior' skills to pursue more intentional and meaningful lives. In so doing, they lessen the stigma most teens feel when they struggle with common problems, such as rumors, loneliness, and harsh criticism from others. My hope for this book is that it will become a textbook for high school and college students all over the world."

—Patricia J. Robinson, PhD, coauthor of *The Mindfulness and Acceptance Workbook for Depression* and *Real Behavior Change in Primary Care*

get out of your mind & into your life for teens

a guide to living an extraordinary life

JOSEPH V. CIARROCHI, PhD
LOUISE HAYES, PhD
ANN BAILEY, MA

Instant Help Books
A Division of New Harbinger Publications, Inc.

Publisher's Note

This publication is designed to provide accurate and authoritative information in regard to the subject matter covered. It is sold with the understanding that the publisher is not engaged in rendering psychological, financial, legal, or other professional services. If expert assistance or counseling is needed, the services of a competent professional should be sought.

Distributed in Canada by Raincoast Books

Copyright © 2012 by Joseph V. Ciarrochi, Louise L. Hayes, and Ann Bailey
    Instant Help Books
    New Harbinger Publications, Inc.
    5674 Shattuck Avenue
    Oakland, CA 94609
    www.newharbinger.com

Cover design by Amy Shoup
Interior illustrations by Sara Christian
Game of Life illustrated by Tegan Spink
Edited by Jasmine Star
Acquired by Catharine Meyers

Library of Congress Cataloging in Publication Data on file

Printed in the United States of America

14   13   12

10   9   8   7   6   5   4   3   2   1   First printing

To Grace and Vincent

May you always find the warrior inside you—AB and JC

To Jackson and Darcy

After all, youth is the moment. Live boldly—LH

Contents

foreword

Whenever you learn to do something complex, like drive a car, no one expects you to just start doing it, learning everything by trial and error. That's why there's driver's ed. If you had to learn to drive just by trial and error, you might try to drive right into a tight parallel parking spot, rather than backing in at an angle. Without some guidance, you might misjudge the distance between your car and another car as you merge into traffic, perhaps with disastrous consequences.

Consider this book a driver's education course for living.

Classroom instruction on how to drive can't do everything—real skill in anything comes only with experience. A person learning to drive might at first use a mental checklist to remember to look to the left and right at a stop sign, or to look in the rearview and side mirrors before passing. Eventually, all of that will be done smoothly and instinctively. A driver's ed class can't do the practicing part for you, but it can help you begin the learning process on the right foot.

This book is about the most complex thing you possess—your own mind. We get a little "driver's education" about our own minds from what others tell us, but it turns out that a lot of conventional advice is pretty far off from what really works. There is a science of psychology, and careful research has regularly arrived at conclusions that go almost in the opposite direction of what the culture, our friends, or the media tell us to do. That's a problem. If behavioral science is right, it means we tend to practice the wrong moves, and practice them so frequently that they become instinctive.

Here is an example. Emotions are sometimes painful. By trial and error, we can easily learn to do things that make that pain go away for a while. If we are afraid of giving a talk in a class, we can take another class, or feign illness, or talk our way out of it, or pretend we don't feel like it. Success in any of these will make the fear go down temporarily—but, ironically, they will all subtly increase the power of fear over our lives. All methods for avoiding painful feelings do that, even the less obvious methods such as pretending not to feel fear, because they all contain the deep message that fear is something to be afraid of.

This book teaches a counterintuitive alternative that has been developed and tested by behavioral scientists: admit the fear, take time to feel it with a sense of genuine curiosity, and then carry it as you might carry your wallet in your back pocket, without letting it dominate over values-based actions. That approach allows us to learn what there is to learn from fear, while also gradually decreasing the power of fear over our lives.

You don't have to trust scientists about these things. You can trust your own experience, because the new skills in this book will pay off very quickly. Once you learn the skills, you can feel yourself becoming more skillful and agile in much the same way that a driver practicing good driving skills quickly notices that her driving is becoming more natural, fluid, and effective.

I wrote the original *Get Out of Your Mind and Into Your Life,* and it made a lot of sense to me to bring this work to teens in a new way, with examples and methods that fit the challenges teens are facing. These three authors are experts in working with teens and, after reading this book, it seems even clearer to me that this was the right thing to do. I recognize the similarity between the issues faced by some of the teens I've worked with and the issues addressed in the vignettes in this book. The authors have cut out unimportant material and presented what is central in a clear and accessible way. The language is direct. The authors don't talk down to you, the reader.

One of the most important things about this "driver's education course for living" is that it does not try to tell you where to go, any more than your driver's ed teacher will tell you *where* to drive once you get your license. Rather, it is focused on how to get there. Teenagers are used to being told what to do by adults, and there is not a need for a book that does more of that. This book aims to help you live your life your way. That sense you have of wanting to live free will be your ally in reading and using it. The book asks what you care about and tries to get in contact with your deeper wisdom. In a sense, you need to decide whose life this is anyway— whether it's yours or whether it belongs to the thoughts and feelings that have been programmed into you.

That is what human freedom is all about. It is the same issue every human being faces, but if you are a teenager it is exciting and wonderful that you have in your hands a book that will encourage you to examine your values early in life and to learn how to use this mind of yours, instead of having it use you.

—Steven C. Hayes
  Professor of Psychology, University of Nevada
  Author of *Get Out of Your Mind and Into Your Life*

acknowledgments

We would like to thank the entire contextual behavioral science community for their willingness to share and provide support. We would also like to thank the New Harbinger staff, and especially Jasmine Star for all her edits and Sara Christian for her illustrations.

introduction: this book is for you

Our deepest fear is not that we are inadequate. Our deepest fear is that we are powerful beyond measure. It is our light, not our darkness, that most frightens us. We ask ourselves, Who am I to be brilliant, gorgeous, handsome, talented, fabulous? *Actually, who are you not to be?*

—Marianne Williamson

There aren't many teenagers who want to open a book like this one, let alone go on to read it. There is a big possibility that an adult in your life asked you to read this, said it might help you, or said there's something wrong with you and this book will fix you. And there's also a big chance that you seriously doubt whether that adult understands you at all. We bet you think this book won't change one single thing.

How do we know?

Well, this book is based on two things: the science behind human behavior, and our experience of working with a lot of teenagers. While we don't know you or your problems, we have listened to what a lot of other teenagers have told us, and we've also learned from what the research shows. We know that most teenagers don't expect a book to help and that they think the adults in their life are way out of touch.

But life is full of surprises. And if you're willing to read on, we hope this little book will offer something that surprises you.

School requires that you spend years studying math, science, geography, literature, and so on. But think about this: How much time do you spend learning human knowledge, about how to deal with difficult thoughts and feelings? How much time do you spend developing knowledge about *you*—an individual who has wants, needs, interests, and a voice that deserves to be heard?

This book is about developing your knowledge of what it means to be a human being and how to cultivate inner strength. Along the way, we'll look at the battle that goes on within each human being. You'll learn about your struggle to understand yourself, to know your thoughts and feelings, and to manage fear and doubt. You'll learn how to move into your life with strength—the strength of a warrior.

We'll also help you explore the secrets and passions within you. You'll discover your strengths, recognize and celebrate what it means to be you, learn more about friendship and relationships, and explore how you can live your dreams. There's no better time to discover this than now!

As you read on, please keep something important in mind: No matter how you came to be holding this book, it is not for others—not for the person or people who say you should read it—this book is for *you*. Our greatest hope is that it helps you on your journey toward living your dreams.

Part 1

Getting Started

Although I'm only fourteen, I know quite well what I want,...I have my opinions, my own ideas and principles, and although it may sound pretty mad from an adolescent, I feel more of a person than a child, I feel quite independent of anyone.

—Anne Frank

Chapter 1

what if everybody is hiding a secret?

Every man has his secret sorrows which the world knows not.

—Henry Wadsworth Longfellow

One of the best ways to develop your knowledge about life is to take a peek at the battles other people face. What are they going through? What are they struggling with?

In this chapter we'll introduce you to several teenagers and their battles. See whether you can relate their struggles to some of the things you've been going through. Take some time to think about whether any of their stories are similar to your own experience. You'll find that by learning to observe another person's struggles, you can become better at understanding your own.

• *The Loser*

I was a teenage loser. I was a guy with no social skills who didn't know how to make and keep friends, didn't know how to protect myself from bullies, and didn't know how to talk to girls. I spent a lot of time escaping into fantasy— daydreaming, playing video games, and listening to music by myself.

I couldn't talk to my mom. She lived somewhere else and never called. I felt like I couldn't talk to my dad. He was so busy with his own stuff

that he didn't have much time for me. He had no idea that I got picked on. He didn't know about the time that an older kid chased me home from school. The only time he noticed me was when I got into trouble. One time a kid was teasing me about my dirty sneakers and just wouldn't stop. He kept calling me "Clorox, Clorox." I got so angry but didn't know what to do, and finally I just hit him in the face. The kid lost a tooth and I got expelled. My dad yelled at me and grounded me, but he didn't ask me why I got in the fight in the first place.

I struggled as a teenager. I pretended that everything was okay and that I didn't care about anything. I got terrible grades and eventually flunked out of school. I thought about committing suicide.

• *The Girl Who Disappeared*

I always wondered what it would be like to disappear in a puff of smoke. Everyone would be left behind saying,"What happened? She was here just a minute ago. We don't know where she went. It seems like she's left the planet!"

I wanted to disappear, and pretty much any way of doing so would have been fine. Maybe I could die instantly in an accident or even fall down a rabbit hole like Alice. I would have done anything if it would have gotten me out of my life.

So I dropped out of school and disappeared into my bedroom. I escaped through music and the posters on my wall. I loved it there. Who needs to live in the real world anyway? I spent years in that room, where I didn't have to face school, homework, adults, or bullies who would punch me in the face, sneak up behind me and tear my hair out by the roots, or spread rumors about me. No one could hurt me in my room. And no one knew why I went there; that was my secret.

I had everything I needed in that bedroom—almost. There was just one problem: my shame was in there with me. After all, only losers can't cope with life, right?

• *The Girl Who Fooled Them All*

I was a popular girl. I wore trendy clothes and hung out with the right people. Anybody who looked at me would have thought that I had everything.

I had them fooled. Every day of my life was filled with the terror of being found out as a fraud. I secretly believed that there was something wrong with me and that I just had everyone convinced otherwise, at least for the moment. At some level, I admired the kids who were isolated. At least they could survive on their own.

I lived in fear and had a hard time eating or sleeping. I would spend three weekends finding the "right" pair of white school sneakers, down to the pattern on the rubber sole, just so I could bear to walk through the school gate. I spent days thinking about every syllable, gesture, and word that came out of the mouths of my so-called friends: What did he mean by that? Why didn't she look at me when she said hi? On and on it went, year after year. It was exhausting.

That was the game. You had to be funnier, louder, skinnier, better—but not too much better. I had to walk a fine line. I had to be just good enough. And the most important rule? Never let anyone see your fear. Yet I was so afraid that I was always on the verge of panic. I hated the way my hair, skin, and body looked every moment. I felt so awkward. The worst thing was that I didn't have the first clue about who I was. And I hated myself for it.

How Did Their Battles End?

Fast-forward a few years (okay, a lot of years). Those three teenagers eventually graduated from college, found friends, and found love. Today their lives are still hard in a lot of ways, but they have a better idea of who they are, and they're living according to what's important to them.

Those three people are the authors of this book: Joseph, Louise, and Ann.

When we were teenagers, we thought everybody else had an easy time of it. Each of us thought we were the only person struggling. We were wrong—so wrong. Eventually, we all studied psychology to fix what we thought was broken in us. But in the process, we discovered that everybody struggles. Even the most successful people have many unhappy experiences, in addition to their positive experiences. In fact, human emotions shift all the time, minute by minute, hour by hour, and day by day. Everybody experiences emotional pain, whether in the form of fear, sadness, shame, or self-doubt. We all struggle to find and build friendships. We all struggle with love, and we all fear rejection. We all want to look strong and cool on the outside, even if we feel weak and terrible on the inside.

Most people look happy on the outside because society teaches us to put on a happy face. Everybody tends to keep their fears a secret, so we don't get the chance to learn that others are struggling too. This is what we mean by everybody having the same secret. Everybody struggles at some point in life, and everybody seeks to hide this struggle from others.

If there's one key thing we hope you'll get from this book, it's this: that you can live your way. You can develop your knowledge about yourself, about people, and about your possibilities, and this will help you create a life that lets you express your talents and interests. Don't ever let anybody tell you otherwise. When people tell you that you can't live your way, don't believe them.

The Wrap-Up

We want you to take heart from knowing that we, the authors of this book, survived our teenage struggles. It took us years, but eventually we found a way through. We learned to hear our own voices over the noise of people telling us what we should and shouldn't do.

This book is about helping you hear your own voice—and helping you do that now, instead of many years in the future, like we did. So take a little time right now to think about who you are and who you want to become. Then read on. Turn to the next chapter and open the door to a new way of living.

Chapter 2

becoming a mindful warrior

May we go to the places that scare us. May we lead the life of a warrior.

—Pema Chödrön

This book is designed to help you become stronger and develop skills that we call mindful warrior skills. We get that this might sound a little weird right now. What is a mindful warrior, anyway? Well, it isn't someone who runs out onto the field of battle like a maniac. It isn't someone who acts impulsively and aggressively. And it isn't someone who's cold and calculating, like a psychopath.

Let's break down what it really means: "Mindful" means paying attention, on purpose and with curiosity. And "warrior" means acting with energy and courage and pursuing what you care about. So when you put the two together, a mindful warrior is someone who has learned about his or her mind, who knows how to act with courage, and who tries to live according to what he or she cares about, or values.

Sounds pretty cool, doesn't it?

We don't expect you to have all of the skills you need to be a mindful warrior yet, or even to fully understand how you can learn them. However, as you progress through this book, you'll learn about these skills and get a lot of opportunities to practice them.

Mindful Warriors Are BOLD

Mindful warriors use four key skills, which you can remember using the acronym BOLD:

Breathing deeply and slowing down

Observing

Listening to your values

Deciding on actions and doing them

Those skills may sound pretty easy, and you might wonder whether they can really help. There's only one way to find out: Try them. Try them as you work through this book. This isn't a book to just read. It's a step-by-step guide. Throughout the book there are exercises for you to do. Some will seem easy, some will seem hard, and some will seem downright silly. (Silly can be fun, though, right?)

The fact of the matter is, BOLD skills will help you deal with your emotions more effectively. They'll allow you to stay committed to what you care about and create the life you want for yourself. So let's look at them a little more closely to give you a better idea of where we're headed.

Breathing deeply and slowing down. Think of your breath as a ship's anchor. It can help you stay where you want to stay, even when emotional forces are trying to pull you out to sea. We all breathe every second of every day, yet we don't always realize that the breath is a great source of strength and stability. Chapter 4 will teach you about mindful breathing and other skills for finding inner stillness.

Observing. Once you've anchored yourself by breathing deeply and slowing down, you can use observation skills to notice what you're feeling and thinking. Observing your thoughts and feelings rather than getting caught up in them will help you gain a little distance from them, and this can help keep them from running your life. Self-doubt doesn't have to stop you from succeeding. Fear doesn't have to block you from making friends or finding love. Observing lets you take a step back from difficult feelings so you can choose the path you want to take. Chapters 3 through 9 will teach you observing skills. Master these skills and you'll become the master of yourself.

Listening to your values. A mindful warrior acts with energy. The key question is, what do you want to turn your energy toward? As a doorman said in the book *Fight Club*, "If you don't know what you want, you end up with a lot you don't." Do you know what you want—what you care about in life? A lot of people don't. You probably don't want to be one of those people. Listening to your values means discovering what's important to you in life—what matters to you and how you want to behave toward yourself, in relationships, and in the wider world. Chapters 10 through 13 will help you discover what you care about in all of those areas. You're much more likely to have a rich life and realize your dreams if you live in a way that's true to yourself and your values.

Deciding on actions and doing them. Once you know what you want, you need to choose actions that will take you toward your goals and values and then commit to doing them. This may take courage, because sometimes you have to face your fears in order to do the things you care about. Chapters 11 through 13 will help you convert your values into actions.

Where Will Warrior Skills Take You?

Mindful warriors observe themselves and learn to live with their human flaws. They learn to face their fears, and they develop courage in the process. They know that courage involves more than running into a burning building to rescue someone or getting up the nerve to go skydiving. As author and artist Mary Ann Radmacher says, "Courage doesn't always roar. Sometimes courage is the quiet voice at the end of the day saying, 'I will try again tomorrow.'"

Of course, courage is something you can use every day of your life. As you practice the skills in this book, you'll benefit in many ways:

- When you feel insecure and afraid, you'll still be able to take chances.

- When you feel anger, you'll be able to choose whether or not you want to act angry.

- When you feel tired and unmotivated, you'll still be able to stay committed to what you care about and to take action toward your goals.

- When you experience the mistakes and failure that are part of life, you'll grow stronger.

The Wrap-Up

Mindful warriors adapt to what life throws at them. They don't run. They face life's challenges by calling on their mindful skills, and in this stillness they discover they don't need to be trapped by their thoughts and feelings. They persist in action when it takes them where they want to go, and they're able to change when what they're doing isn't helping their cause. Being mindful brings flexibility in thoughts, feelings, and action.

Mindfulness is the foundation for discovering how to live your way with courage and strength, and your mindfulness will grow stronger as you practice all of the BOLD skills. The opposite of this would be mindlessness, which means doing things without thinking or paying much attention, running away from your own feelings, and not doing what you care about. Mindlessness usually has an inflexible quality.

To help you see which skills you're learning and to guide you in practicing the skills you need to work on, you'll find the following text box at the beginning of chapters 3 through 13, with check marks indicating the skills each chapter focuses on.

BOLD Warrior Skills	
Breathing deeply and slowing down	
Observing	
Listening to your values	
Deciding on actions and doing them	

Part 2

The Battle Within

When we are in the midst of chaos, let go of the need to control it. Be awash in it, experience it in that moment, try not to control the outcome but deal with the flow as it comes.

—Leo Babauta

Chapter 3

beginning the journey

BOLD Warrior Skills	
Breathing deeply and slowing down	
Observing	✓
Listening to your values	
Deciding on actions and doing them	

Midway upon the journey of our life
I found myself within a forest dark,
For the straightforward pathway had been lost.

—Dante Alighieri

We've mentioned that this book is a journey of discovery. You won't go on this journey alone. As you work through this book, two teenagers will travel with you: Jess and Sam. Both are stuck and have been struggling to find their way in life. Throughout the book, you'll see them transform themselves into mindful warriors. But it doesn't happen just by wishing; as you'll see, they have to practice.

We've used our experience in working with teenagers to create these characters. They are composites of various teenagers we've worked with and their journeys. Their stories will show you how other teenagers have come to understand themselves and find their way using mindful warrior skills. We hope this will encourage you to try out the skills.

As you read their stories, observe what they have in common with you. Also notice when they're being mindless versus when they're acting like mindful warriors—that is, paying attention to their feelings, acting with courage, and using BOLD warrior skills.

• *Jess: My Life Is Over!*

Hi, I'm Jess.

It all started last year. Or maybe I should say it all ended. My former best friend, Sally, was madly in love with Josh, but Josh didn't like her—he liked me. One night we were at a party and Sally came in and saw Josh and me talking. She was so mad that she texted me swearing and saying how dare I steal him—he was hers. But he wasn't hers. She had never even gone out with him! And like I said, he liked me.

The next day Sally spread rumors at school that I'd had sex with Josh. Now the whole world thinks they know all about me. As for Josh, he won't even look at me. Even though he knows it's just a rumor—and that I supposedly had sex with him—it's like it was all my fault.

In one crazy moment, I lost my best friend, a boy I liked, and my school life. Oh, man, my life is over, just because of this one thing.

I guess I should tell you about some other stuff too. I'm seventeen. My two brothers and I live with our mom. Our house isn't the best, but it's okay. I have my own room. If you walked into it, you would laugh. The walls and ceiling are almost completely plastered with pictures and posters of musicians, bands, and my favorite TV shows, along with tickets from shows I've been to and some weird things like my broken iPod, which I stuck to the wall too. And then there are my drawings. I'm okay at art.

My room is like a collection representing me. Mom says she'll have to strip the room when I leave home. She once took photos to show her friends, and then she put a sign saying "Caution: Under Demolition" on the door. I think she thought that would make me clean my room, but I didn't, and the sign is still there. I like it that way. We now have a deal: I keep the door shut, and she stays off my case about cleaning my room.

So now it's summer and I'm not going to school. Plus, I can't face my so-called friends. So my life is pretty much me in my room.

• *Sam: How Did It Go So Wrong?*

Hi. My name is Sam. I'm fifteen years old. I've been suspended from school for a week. They say I have trouble with anger. It all started in my freshman year because I didn't fit in. There were a few different groups: the jocks, the in-crowd, and the nerdy guys who had no friends and were into books and stuff. And there was one last group: the tough guys. They ruled the school. They hung together pretty tight and didn't want to let any outsiders in. They spent most of their time insulting people who weren't in their group. Not that I'd ever admit it to anyone, but I was pretty scared of those guys. I didn't want to get in their way.

I had to survive it, but I didn't know how. I was kind of skinny and probably couldn't fend for myself in a fight. I knew it, and before long everyone else would know it too. I realized I had to do something.

The only way to go was to get in with the tough group. Then no one would touch me.

I remember the day I got in with them. There was this guy Dorian, who everyone teased. He was an easy target. Looking back, I feel like crap about what I did. I decided to pretend that Dorian was gay and had a boyfriend named Steve. I made up stories about the stuff that Dorian did with Steve and texted it to some guys at school. When I told the guys what I'd done, they loved it. And from that point on, I was in. From then on, people just expected me to do that sort of stuff. I started acting tough and picking fights because I needed people to be scared of me. Otherwise I'd be a goner. I had to keep it up 24/7.

Dorian's dad filed a complaint against me. They had traced the rumor back to my phone. So now I'm suspended for a week and I don't know what will happen after that. People have been telling me that I'm a bully and really hurt Dorian—that he's had to see a counselor to get over it. I only wanted to fit in, but now I feel like crap. There must be something wrong with me. I feel kind of disgusted with myself, but I wouldn't say that to the guys. I've tried punching and kicking things in the yard, but I'm still angry.

Exercise: Noticing What's Going On with Jess and Sam

Let's do an exercise. Take a minute to think about what's happening for Jess and Sam in these stories. More specifically, observe whether Jess and Sam seem like mindful warriors: Are they persisting in what matters to them? Are they acting with flexibility by observing and working with their thoughts and feelings, or are they acting inflexibly by running from themselves? It's often much easier to see what's going wrong for other people than it is to observe what's happening in your own life. That's why we're having you start practicing observing by looking at the stories of Jess and Sam. Think about their situations, then answer the following questions:

1. How would you sum up their situations? What do you think is happening for Jess and Sam? Think of a few things that are really obvious about each story.

2. Can you sum up how they feel right now in just a few words?

    Here are some possible answers (not necessarily the only correct ones).

Jess

1. Jess was embarrassed at school and among her friends. It wasn't her fault, but she's very unsure what she should do now. At this point, she's isolating herself from friends.

2. She feels like one event ruined her life.

Sam

1. Sam felt afraid and decided to play tough. He started bullying a boy, and now he's suspended.

2. He feels bad about himself and like he's defective. He also feels angry all the time and has tried to vent his anger by punching things.

    Even though their situations are totally different, we think both Jess and Sam are feeling *stuck*, even though that shows up in different ways. They feel stuck in life situations that they don't want to be in, and they're also stuck in their thoughts about how to escape. Their minds are trying to think up ways to get back in control.

Exercise: Noticing What's Going On in Your Story

Before we move on, what's your story? What can you observe about what's going on in your life right now? Take a minute to sum up your travels through life and any battles you might have. Are you like

Jess or more like Sam? Or maybe you aren't like either one of them. Take a few minutes to write your own story and the struggles you're facing, along the lines of what Jess and Sam wrote, in the space below. If you feel stuck(!) about what to write, tell the story of how you ended up reading this book. If you need more space, you can write your story on a separate piece of paper or in your journal.

_____

_____

_____

_____

_____

_____

_____

_____

_____

_____

_____

Now see what you might observe about your story. And when you look over your story, does "stuck" describe how you feel sometimes too? Are you maybe stuck feeling insecure, angry, or fearful? Or maybe you feel trapped by things that have happened to you. If "stuck" or "trapped" don't seem to apply to your situation, maybe another word or two comes to mind to sum up your situation, like "struggling," "unsure," or "afraid."

The Wrap-Up

Feeling stuck is something we humans don't like very much. It's also the perfect time to put mindful warrior skills to use. Why not give it a try? We feel pretty sure that as you work through this book, you'll gradually feel less stuck and start to find life opening up in ways you might not have expected.

Chapter 4

finding your inner stillness

BOLD Warrior Skills	
Breathing deeply and slowing down	✓
Observing	✓
Listening to your values	
Deciding on actions and doing them	

The self must know stillness before it can discover its true song.

—Ralph Blum

In this chapter we'll outline several exercises that can help you stay grounded even in really tough times. All of these techniques help build mindfulness—which is crucial for becoming a mindful warrior! All of them will also help you slow down, observe what's happening, and find stillness. That opens the door to making deliberate choices that reflect your values. This will keep you from getting lost in the storms that are inevitable in life. As with anything in life, the key to success is practice, practice, practice. So don't just read through these exercises. Take the time to do them, and then keep working with them as you continue reading this book.

Exercise: Breathing Mindfully

We know you know how to breathe, but you probably don't know how useful this skill can be for a mindful warrior. In this exercise, we'll teach you how to use your breath in a new way: as an anchor. Think of a ship in an ocean harbor. The ocean is rough and the wind is howling. What keeps the ship from being pulled out of the harbor and lost at sea? An anchor. When a ship drops anchor, it remains in place even in powerful storms.

The way of breathing we'll teach you here is called mindful breathing. It will help you in all sorts of situations. When you notice yourself getting caught up in your thoughts or feelings, mindful breathing can help you find a solid base again. It won't make your thoughts or feelings go away, and that wouldn't be the goal anyway. You need to learn to live—and thrive—with your thoughts and feelings. Mindful breathing will help you stand firm when you feel besieged by storms, whether the storm is inside your body or out in the world. It helps you pause and respond thoughtfully, rather than reacting mindlessly. When you focus on your breath, you can center yourself and find a calm space to decide how you want to live. With practice, you'll find an inner stillness that will allow you to be more flexible in how you handle challenges.

Step 1: Notice Your Breath

Start by just noticing how you're breathing right now. Place one hand on your chest and one hand on your belly. Relax your hands in these positions and observe your breath for a moment. Is the hand on your belly rising when you breathe in, or is the hand on your chest rising? Or maybe it's a bit of both.

We're guessing that you'll find that the hand on your chest is moving more. Most people tend to breathe into their chest. This is normal. What you're about to learn is something slightly different: breathing into your belly.

Step 2: Fill the Balloon

Keep your hands in the same positions and be sure that you're sitting upright. Now we're going to ask you to use your imagination to do something a bit unusual. We want you to imagine that you have a balloon in your belly. When you breathe in, the balloon in your belly inflates and gets bigger, and this makes your belly rise. And when you breathe out, the balloon gets smaller; it deflates and your belly goes down.

When you breathe this way, the hand on your chest shouldn't move very much. It may take some time to get used to breathing this way. You may need to practice, since this is probably different from the way you've been breathing. Just stay with it and keep observing your breath. As you breathe in, the balloon inflates and gets bigger. As you breathe out, the balloon deflates and gets smaller.

Don't feel bad if you have trouble staying focused on your breath. That happens to everybody. Counting as you breathe may help. When you inhale, think, *In, two, three.* Then, when you exhale, think, *Out, two, three.*

Practice breathing this way for at least a minute. After a minute, you might still feel like your emotions are trying to push you around. If so, you practice deep breathing for three minutes or even a bit longer.

Step 3: Practice

Now you just need to practice. To get really good at this skill, you need to practice it at least a few times each week. We recommend that you practice for a few minutes each time and that you practice every day. If you practice when things are calm, you'll find it easier to breathe this way when times get tough.

The beauty of mindful breathing is that you can practice it anywhere, anytime. If you're waiting for the bus, think about the balloon expanding in your belly when you breathe in and deflating when you breathe out. Likewise, when you're sitting in class or listening to music, use it as an opportunity to take a few mindful belly breaths.

Plus, this kind of deep breathing is the foundation for many other exercises that will help you become more mindful, or curious and connected to the present moment. The exercises that follow are just a few of the possibilities. With all of them, it's a good idea to start by doing some mindful breathing for a minute or two.

Any time you feel angry, afraid, stressed, or upset, remember to take a few mindful breaths. You'll be amazed at how effective it is at helping you calm down. It's one of the best skills a warrior can have. Actually, it's one of the best skills any human can have.

• *Jess: Finding Stillness Within*

Mindful breathing sounded so lame. I really didn't expect that how I was breathing could make one bit of difference. How can it? I've been breathing since I was born! But I really liked the idea of being a warrior—Jess, Warrior Princess!—so I decided to give it a try.

Plus, I really want to do something other than sit at home, and at this point I'm willing to try anything. So I started practicing, trying to breathe this way, but I kept getting distracted. So I added in counting to three when I inhale and counting to three when

I exhale, and that helped a little. I've been doing it for a little while each day for a couple of weeks now. The exercise is fine, but I don't feel like it changed me into a mindful warrior. Nothing much seemed to happen—until just now.

I had the biggest fight with Mom. I was shaking all over and felt like I wanted to scream and run away. I sat on my bed and cried really hard. But then I started breathing and counting. It didn't make my angry feelings toward Mom go away, but I did feel less like running away and a tiny bit more in control of myself.

Weathering the Storm

Jess has done a pretty good job of practicing this exercise. And she's right: Mindful breathing doesn't make difficult feelings go away—and it isn't meant to. Rather, it helps you learn to anchor yourself instead of being swept away by your feelings. That's very different from making feelings disappear. So even as she practices mindful breathing, Jess will still feel angry, and she'll also feel a bit more in control of herself. What's great about Jess is that she knows she needs to practice this skill each day when she feels calm so she can develop skills for dealing with tough situations when they come along.

Exercise: Tuning In to Your Body

In this exercise, you'll build on using your breath as an anchor and start developing your observation skills by tuning in to what's going on in your body.

Begin by doing some mindful breathing, taking just a few breaths and filling the balloon each time.

Bring your attention to noticing different parts of your body. First notice your feet, then feel your feet touching the surface beneath them. You might have to wiggle your toes to even know that your feet are there! Take a minute to notice every sensation in your feet. You might observe things like temperature, tightness from shoes, wrinkles in your socks—anything that you notice is fine. Keep breathing mindfully as you notice all of these things.

Next, observe your shoulders and neck. See whether you can notice all the sensations you feel in these areas. See whether you can detect the temperature, your clothes touching your body, or perhaps some tightness in the muscles. Anything you notice is fine. You can wiggle your shoulders if that helps you notice the sensations in these areas.

By now, you probably get the idea of this exercise: Breathe mindfully—slowly and deeply—while also noticing sensations in your body. You can use any part of your body as a focus, or even move through all of the parts of your body sequentially. This exercise strengthens your "mindfulness muscles" and can help you manage during difficult times, like when you're stressed during an exam or when things go wrong.

Exercise: Listening to Music with New Ears

How cool is it that you can develop mindful warrior skills by listening to your favorite tunes? For this exercise, you need to choose a piece of music you love and have listened to a lot. Now you're going to listen to it again, but this time you'll practice being mindful of different parts of the music.

Before you start playing the music, sit down and make yourself comfortable.

Begin by taking a few deep, mindful breaths to anchor yourself. Sit still and count silently *In, two, three. Out, two, three.*

Next, play the music and give it your full attention. Don't do anything else. You may find that your attention wanders from the music. That's fine. It happens to everyone. In fact, that's part of the exercise: noticing that your attention has wandered. Every time that happens, just bring yourself back to the music.

After you've played the song once, you may want to play it again or listen to a different piece of music. (You can do this right away, or try it another time.) Again, give it your full attention. But this time, practice shifting your attention to different parts of the song. For example, first put your full attention on the vocals. Then shift it to the guitar, the keyboard, or another instrument. Then shift it again, to another instrument. You can also observe qualities like rhythm or tempo. Spend about thirty seconds focusing on one aspect of the song and then shift to another. This will give you excellent practice in observing. If you notice that your mind has wandered, bring your attention back to the music. That's all you need to do to practice this skill.

Other Ways of Building Observation Skills

Mindfulness can be practiced in all kinds of fun ways. For example, you can practice mindful eating by devoting your attention to your food with a sense of curiosity. Use all five of your senses when you eat. Look at your food, taste it, smell it, touch it, and even try listening to it.

You can do just about anything mindfully. You can do chores, take a walk, take a shower, or play with a pet mindfully.

You can also engage in mindful conversations, paying full attention to the person you're talking with and really trying to understand what the other person is feeling. Being mindful means really listening, whereas thinking about what you're going to say next is mindless. You'll be surprised at how helpful mindful listening can be in strengthening friendships. Pick a friend you'd like get to know better and ask that person one of the questions below, then listen mindfully as your friend replies:

- What's the bravest thing you've ever done?

- What's your biggest goal for this year?

- What do you spend most of your money on?

- What's the best compliment you've ever received?

- What's the most fun you've had in the last year?

- What's a subject you wish you knew more about?

The Wrap-Up

Breathing mindfully and observing—these simple skills are the key to becoming a mindful warrior. Your breath is always there, available to you. Any time you get caught up in your mind and are feeling extremely emotional and maybe out of control, tune in to your breath. Just notice it, breathe deeply, and count, *In, two, three. Out, two, three.* It's as simple as that. Be sure to practice all of the exercises in this chapter often, because breathing and observing are skills you'll be using throughout the rest of the book—and throughout your life!

Chapter 5

observing the battle within

BOLD Warrior Skills	
Breathing deeply and slowing down	✓
Observing	✓
Listening to your values	
Deciding on actions and doing them	

We can spend our whole lives escaping from the monsters of our minds.

—Pema Chödrön

Mindful warriors don't fight for the sake of fighting. Rather, they fight for what's important, for what matters to them. They fight for their values.

This chapter is about how we humans tend to fight our emotions, which can seem like inner monsters, and try to make them go away. We'll teach you to use your observing skills to notice your own battle with emotions. If you've ever hated the way you felt or tried to make feelings go away, this chapter is for you.

The truth is that feelings and thoughts are connected. But for the purposes of writing about them and helping you untangle what's going on inside, we'll focus on feelings in chapters 5 and 6 and thoughts in chapters 7 and 8.

Understanding Emotions

First, let's look at what emotions are about. Everybody has them, but most people don't really understand why we have them or how they work. Many psychologists believe that humans have nine basic feelings:

- Joy
- Fear
- Anger

- Shock
- Love
- Disgust

- Sadness
- Guilt
- Curiosity

Of course, each emotion comes in a variety of "flavors," and sometimes we experience blends of emotions. But for now, let's just consider these nine basic emotions. Look over the list again. Which ones have you been taught are "good," and which are thought of as "bad"?

If you're like most people, you said that joy, love, and curiosity are good and the other six are bad. And because it's perfectly natural for us to want to avoid "bad" feelings, we try to ignore or get rid of them.

Take a moment to think about "bad" feelings that you'd rather not have. Do you want to get rid of embarrassment or fear? Do you want to avoid sadness or guilt? If you said yes to any of these, welcome to the human condition. Everybody tries to get rid of "bad" feelings—adults, teens, and even young children. But there's a catch. Have you ever noticed that the more you try not to feel sad, the more down you feel, or that the more you try not to feel worried, the more anxious you feel?

It's kind of weird, though, don't you think—only having nine basic feelings, yet trying not to have six of them and then finding that we feel them even more when we don't want to? It's like we're fighting an internal war against most of our emotions.

• *Jess and Sam: Fighting the Feelings War*

Here's the way we see the feelings war being played out in the lives of Jess and Sam:

Enemy: Badsadmad, the feelings monster

Aim: Eliminate the monster

Weapon: Rope

Location: The top of a deep pit

The battle is set: a tug-of-war, with Jess and Sam on one side of the pit and Badsadmad, the monster of negative feelings, on the other. By pulling the monster into the pit, Jess and Sam can be free of fear, doubt, or sadness. All that's needed is one massive effort to pull the monster into the pit and get rid of it. The prize is fantastic: never having to feel bad again.

Sometimes the monster seems to be winning. Sometimes Jess and Sam seem to be winning. They give the battle everything they've got, pulling as hard as they can. They battle for hours, days, weeks. But there's a problem. The more Jess and Sam pull, the more tired they become. Meanwhile, it seems the monster only becomes stronger.

If they win, the war will be over for good. Monstrous feelings banished forever. But it's hard work, and it might take years of effort. Can Jess and Sam do it?

We'll return to the feelings war later. For now, let's look at ways you might try to win in your own feelings battles.

The Battle for Control

We all try so hard to avoid "bad" feelings, and this shows up in a lot of different ways. For example, some people bully others because they don't want to feel insecure. Other people surf the Internet for hours to avoid having to think about something unpleasant, like an upcoming exam. Some feel insecure in social situations, so they choose to avoid people altogether. And others are so afraid of feeling like a loser that they avoid taking on challenges; they'd rather play it safe than play for higher stakes.

Despite the countless ways that people try to avoid feeling bad, nothing seems to work. People still freak out when they have to give a speech. They still feel like the world is ending when a friendship falls apart. They still feel ashamed when they fail. They still feel angry or humiliated when someone insults them. Many people secretly believe that they're deeply flawed. Even now, as you read this, someone somewhere is thinking about suicide. Someone is crying. Someone is having hateful thoughts toward someone else. Someone is feeling ashamed. Why can't we make these thoughts and feelings go away? Why can't we defeat our inner monsters? Maybe Sam's story can help answer those questions.

• *Sam: Trying to Control Feelings*

I've been sitting around now for almost a week. Being suspended from school is killing me. I just can't stand myself. Every time I stop for a minute, I start to think about all of the bad things I've done. I hate myself. More than anything, I just want that horrible feeling of guilt to go away. Guilt is like some serial killer from a movie. Just when you think you've gotten rid of him, he sneaks up and grabs you. I feel like I can't breathe.

Try to keep it down is what I say to myself. But pushing away my feelings is pretty much a full-time job. Basically, I just try to keep busy.

Today I took my skateboard out to the park and rode hard—so hard that I was drenched in sweat. That made me feel okay for a while—until some dude looked at me sideways. I yelled rude comments in his direction to keep him in his place.

On my way home, I went by the mall. I saw Sandy, a girl who lives down the street from me. I like her, so I smiled. She smiled back and started to walk in my direction. I freaked out because I knew that if she started talking to me, she'd realize I'm a loser.

I turned around, jumped on my skateboard, and got out of there. Once I was a safe distance away, I slowed down. I hate myself for being so weak. I wondered what's wrong with me. I can't even talk to a girl, let alone get anywhere with one! I put on my iPod and blasted heavy metal through my head. Then I slammed my fist into a fence. That took the edge off—for a while.

Exercise: Observing Sam's Battle

When you look at Sam's afternoon, he experienced a number of difficult feelings and he reacted to these feelings by doing various things to try to control them. He tried skating hard, running from Sandy, blasting his music, and punching the fence. In the space below, list the difficult feelings you think Sam was trying to stop and whether his strategies made things better for Sam.

Sam's control strategy	Sam's feelings	Did it help?
Keeping busy		
Skating hard		
Running from Sandy		
Blasting his music		
Punching the fence		

Exercise: Observing Your Own Battle for Control

Mindful warriors learn to pick their battles carefully. As you practice the skills in this book, you'll learn how to do this. The first step is to take a look at what you do when you're trying to control your feelings. Start by taking a look at the feelings below. Do you ever want to shift the feelings on the left to the feelings on the right? Do you ever try to do that?

Afraid	→	Fearless
Insecure	→	Self-assured
Sad	→	Happy
Embarrassed	→	Cool and confident

As we mentioned, people use a lot of different strategies to try to push away negative feelings. One way to look at these strategies is to divide them into two groups: inner strategies and outer strategies. Inner strategies are things you do to fight the monster inside, like when Sam was trying not to think by blasting his brain with music. Outer strategies are things you do outside your body to fight your feelings, like when Sam ran away from Sandy.

Take a minute to look through the lists of inner and outer strategies below, then check off the things you sometimes do to avoid negative feelings. Next, think of people you know extremely well and what you might have seen them do to battle their feelings, then check those off in the right-hand column. (We're having you do this because it's good to know that you aren't the only person who uses these strategies.)

	I do this sometimes	People I know do this sometimes
Inside strategies		
Pushing negative feelings out of your mind		
Obsessing about other things		
Eating too much		
Sleeping to avoid feelings		
Exercising too much		
Procrastinating		
Daydreaming to avoid feelings		
Avoiding being with people		
Criticizing yourself		
Drinking alcohol or using drugs to block feelings		
Playing video games, watching TV, or using the computer to avoid feelings		
Outer strategies		
Getting mad at people		
Pretending to be strong		
Acting like you don't care		
Trying to be invisible		
Making a big deal about how hurt you are		
Being "super-nice" and trying to please everyone		
Excluding people from your social network		
Saying mean things about others		
Teasing other people		

Now go back over the lists, and for each box you checked for strategies you sometimes use, consider this important question: Does that strategy work for very long? Does it make your life worse sometimes?

We hope that looking over these lists of what you do and what other people do will help you understand that battling and controlling feelings doesn't work so well. And think about it: if it did work, strong feelings wouldn't really be a problem, would they?

Exercise: Experimenting with Control

We don't want to teach you a bunch of rules about what you should do about your feelings. As a mindful warrior, you'll learn to trust your own experience and figure out what you need to do in your unique situation. But just in case you still think control might be the way to go, let's do three quick experiments.

Experiment 1

Imagine a chocolate cake. Try to make it as real as possible. Make it a beautiful, warm chocolate cake, with gooey chocolate sauce oozing over it. Then imagine you're about to eat a big slice of it.

Ready for the hard part? For the next three minutes, you are *not allowed* to think about chocolate cake. Time yourself. Each time you think about that rich, gooey, delicious chocolate cake, put a check mark in one of the boxes below.

Did you find this experiment difficult? Most people do. Even if you succeeded, you probably found it took a lot of effort. You probably had to concentrate on something else really hard. Now imagine doing that every waking hour. It would be exhausting, and you couldn't get much done. Yet that's exactly what many people do to avoid feelings.

Experiment 2

Take a minute to look around and choose a spot on the floor, the wall, or the ground. Really fix that spot in your mind so you can come back to it at a moment's notice. Ready for the experiment? We want you to fall deeply, madly in love with that spot. (Yes, we do mean that we want you to fall in love with that spot!)

Take your time. Really work hard to fall in love with that spot. Imagine that you want to build a shrine to it and tell all of your friends how great it is because you love it so much.

Did you succeed? We're guessing you didn't. It just goes to show that it's hard to force yourself to have positive feelings. You really can't make yourself fall in love or feel happy.

Experiment 3

Imagine this: We'll give you $100 million if you can do two things. First, you have to get rid of all of the garbage in your house for one week. Could you do it? We're guessing you could. Second, you have to get rid of all of your negative feelings—sadness, fear, frustration, insecurity, whatever—for one whole week. Could you do it? Imagine all the pressure you would feel. You stand to win $100 million! How could you not have feelings like stress? If you said you couldn't get rid of negative feelings, you're not alone. You simply can't get rid of feelings like you get rid of garbage.

The Bottom Line

You can't force yourself *not* to have feelings or thoughts. The more you try to, the less likely you are to succeed. It's like there are two rules:

- **The rule outside your body and mind:** *If you want to get rid of something that you don't like (garbage, for example), you usually can.*

- **The rule inside your body and mind:** *If you want to get rid of feelings and thoughts that you don't like, you usually can't.*

The Wrap-Up

We humans battle to try to keep from feeling bad. But as you saw in this chapter, while avoiding difficult feelings might help you feel better in the short run, it doesn't work in the long run. Why? Because while we can get rid of bad stuff in the outside world (like garbage), it's a lot harder—and usually impossible—to get rid of stuff in the inside world (like fear).

We can't leave this chapter without revisiting what all of this means for Sam and Jess. They began this chapter in a battle—a *feelings* war—fighting against the monster Badsadmad and trying to win ultimate control over their feelings. But can they ever really win? Isn't there always the chance for more bad feelings in the future? Maybe this is a mindless battle. If they keep fighting, maybe they'll need to fight forever. Read on to find out how Jess and Sam became mindful warriors and learned to work with their feelings instead of fighting against them.

Chapter 6

making the winning move

BOLD Warrior Skills	
Breathing deeply and slowing down	✓
Observing	✓
Listening to your values	
Deciding on actions and doing them	✓

Notice that the stiffest tree is most easily cracked, while the bamboo or willow survives by bending with the wind.

—Bruce Lee

In this chapter we'll help you continue to sharpen your observing skills, but we'll also start to take a look at deciding skills: choosing actions and then following through on doing them. When it comes to feelings, these two skills work well together. The first step is to observe—to notice when you're battling your feelings. Then you can decide whether to continue the battle or choose to do something else.

Most people are so used to battling their feelings that they think it's the only way to respond. But think about it: A warrior with only one strategy isn't a very good warrior. Maybe it's time to learn some other responses. Let's take a look at how this played out for Jess and Sam.

- ### *Jess and Sam: Discovering That Willingness Wins*

Let's return to the battleground.

Enemy: Badsadmad, the feelings monster

Aim: Eliminate the monster

Weapon: Rope

Location: The top of a deep pit

Jess and Sam are fighting hard, each trying to pull the feelings monster into the pit. If they succeed, they will gain ultimate control over their feelings. They'll never have to feel deep, dark feelings like fear, anger, or embarrassment again.

Jess is pulling hard, trying to beat the monster, but she feels like she isn't making any progress. In fact, sometimes she's slipping closer to the edge herself. Over her shoulder she hears others, warriors who are no longer fighting this battle. They've been going about their lives and are sharing stories of adventure and fun.

Sam is much stronger. It seems like he's pulled the monster closer to the edge—so close

that the edge of the pit begins to crumble and break. But Sam is sweaty, exhausted, and shaking. How much longer can he go on?

Suddenly, Jess gets a completely new idea. With a wide-eyed expression on her face, she exclaims, "Of course, that's it!" She drops her end of the rope and gazes at the Badsadmad with curiosity. The monster jumps up and down and yells, "Listen to me! I can make you feel afraid. I can make you fear for your life!" But the spell has been broken. Jess has realized that she can win the battle without fighting. The answer seems so simple and yet was so hard to see: Just let go of the rope. Why didn't anyone teach me that? she wonders. Finally, she sees that the feelings monster can't really hurt her. Sure, it's mean and menacing, but what can it do, really?

She stands her ground and confronts the monster: "Yell mean things at me? Is that it? You've got nothing else?"

Then she offers Sam some advice: "There's another way. You win by not fighting."

"You win by letting go of the rope?"

"Yeah. The mindful warrior move is to be strong by not fighting yourself."

The Alternative to Fighting

All of the BOLD skills can help you work with unpleasant feelings. When those feelings show up, the first thing to do is breathe deeply. Then observe your feelings. When you take a close look, it's likely that those feelings are telling you something about your values. And once you can observe your feelings, you have a choice about how to deal with them. Basically, you have two options:

1. Be unwilling to have the feelings. Try to get rid of them.

2. Be willing to have the feelings. Let the feelings come and go, especially when this allows you to do something that's important to you. For example, you might be willing to experience fear in order to make a presentation in class or ask someone out on a date.

Which option you choose is totally up to you. Since you may not have a lot of experience with option 2, here's an exercise where you can see what it's like.

Exercise: Being Willing to Be Out of Breath

To do this exercise, you need a timer that can display seconds, such as a watch or the clock on a phone or computer. There are two parts to the exercise.

Part 1

Hold your breath for as long as you can. Start now, and when you're finished, write down how long you held your breath.

Time 1: I held my breath for _____ seconds.

Part 2

Now do the same thing again, but this time be willing to have discomfort and difficult feelings, and also put your observing skills to work. Here's what we want you to do:

1. Take a few deep breaths and slow down.

2. Hold your breath and notice any discomfort. Just let the discomfort be there. Don't try to get rid of it. Just look at your experience with curiosity.

Time 2: I held my breath for _____ seconds.

This exercise isn't about holding your breath longer. It's about being willing to experience discomfort. You might have held your breather longer or shorter the second time. Shorter or longer—neither is right or wrong.

Now take a couple of minutes to describe your experience during this exercise. Did your discomfort about holding your breath tend to come and go? When did your level of discomfort increase or decrease?

_____

_____

_____

How did your mind try to persuade you to breathe before you really had to?

_____

_____

_____

This exercise shows that willingness isn't just about gritting your teeth and enduring tough feelings. Willingness involves observing feelings as they come and go without getting caught up in them. To get an idea of how willingness plays out in real life, let's look at Sam's situation and how he chooses to be willing and use BOLD skills in the service of something he wants.

- ## *Sam: Being Willing*

I can't get Sandy out of my mind—that girl I ran away from the other day at the mall. She actually smiled at me. She's really hot! Whenever I've heard her say anything, she's always so nice. I wish she were my girlfriend. The thing is, every time she's around I get so nervous that I run the other way—or pretend to be cool and act like I don't notice her.

I want to get to know her. But I don't want to be nervous around her. So I just avoid her. But I can't get her out of my mind… I'm going around in circles. I'm stuck.

I've noticed that the stuff I do to avoid all of these feelings, like run away or act cool, makes me feel better for a while, but then later I just hate myself for not having the nerve to talk to her. I just can't seem to forget about her, and it's getting worse.

Since I haven't been getting anywhere with my same old approach, I decided to see about using those goofy BOLD skills. They're okay, I guess. They feel kind of funny, but they do seem to clear my head a bit.

And I've made another decision: Today I'm going to talk to Sandy even if I feel scared. I'm going to say hi. If I start feeling like I'll freak out, I'll do some of that mindful breathing. And even if it feels like I'm going to die, I'm doing it. I'm sick of waiting. I'm not going to let my mind scare me out of talking to her!

A Formula for Willingness

Sam felt extremely nervous about saying hello to Sandy. In the past, he let those feelings push him around and avoided talking to her. That helped his nervousness go away, but it lost him the chance to make friends with Sandy. That was a huge cost. So Sam finally decided to be willing to feel nervous and talk to Sandy anyway.

This is what using BOLD skills looks like for everyone: being willing to have a feeling, observing it, and choosing to do what you care about.

In chapters 11 through 13, we'll help you clarify your values. Knowing what you care about is key to the kind of commitment that allows for willingness. For now, just keep this simple formula for willingness in mind:

I am willing to have _____ (fear, insecurity, sadness, anger, and so on),

in order to _____ (do something you care about).

Exercise: Understanding Willingness

Negative feelings and desires are often connected. As you saw with Sam, sometimes you can't avoid difficult feelings without also giving up doing things that are important to you. So you could try to get rid of negative feelings if you want (good luck with that!), but that will probably mean that you have to give up things you really want in life. To illustrate this point, take a moment to answer the following four willingness questions.

1. To strive for success, you risk all of the following:

    - *Feeling like a failure sometimes*

    - *Feeling sad about losing*

    - *Feeling stupid*

    - *Feeling disappointed*

      Are you willing to strive for success anyway?

2. To search for love, you risk all of the following:
    - *Feeling rejected*

    - *Feeling lonely*

    - *Feeling insecure*

    - *Feeling vulnerable*

      Are you willing to search for love anyway?

3. To be a friend, you risk all of the following:

    - *Feeling let down*

    - *Feeling disappointed*

    - *Feeling embarrassed when you do something you didn't mean to do*

    - *Getting your feelings hurt*

      Are you willing to be a friend anyway?

4. To have an adventure, you risk all of the following:

- *Feeling disappointed that it wasn't as good as you had hoped*

- *Feeling out of control sometimes*

- *Feeling sad when the adventure comes to an end*

- *Learning unpleasant things about life, like about challenges or dealing with unexpected difficulties*

    Are you willing to have an adventure anyway?

Each time you answer yes to questions like this, you give yourself the chance to expand your life and discover new things. Each time you answer no and try not to have certain feelings, you restrict yourself. You can't say no to your feelings without also saying no to your life.

Here's a list of some things that teens commonly care about. From this list, choose one thing that you'd like to do but find a bit difficult. Then plug it into the willingness formula below. Would you be willing to have negative feelings in order to do that thing? Remember, this is about what matters to *you*, so only you can answer the question.

- *Saying something assertive to a friend*

- *Introducing yourself to someone you want to go out with*

- *Standing up to a bully*

- *Entering a competition, such as chess or sports*

- *Pushing yourself to perform, like in sports or scholastics*

- *Studying for a difficult exam*

- *Giving a talk in front of class*

    I am willing to have _____ (fear, insecurity, sadness, anger, and so on),

    in order to _____ (do something you care about).

The Wrap-Up

The battle within is about trying to control unpleasant feelings, such as fear and insecurity. Chapters 5 and 6 have shown that you have two options:

1. Fight the feelings.

2. Use BOLD skills and be willing to have difficult feelings in the service of something you care about.

Keep in mind that there is no right or wrong choice. Sometimes you'll choose willingness; sometimes you won't. It all comes down to what you want your life to be about. Think of willingness as taking a leap. You get to decide how far to jump. You can take a small leap—just doing something fairly easy. Or you can take a large leap and face a scary challenge.

If you do choose to take a leap, you'll want to put all of the BOLD skills to work: Breathe deeply and slow down; observe your feelings in a curious and open way; listen to your values; and decide to do what you care about.

Chapter 7

meeting the machine

BOLD Warrior Skills	
Breathing deeply and slowing down	✓
Observing	✓
Listening to your values	
Deciding on actions and doing them	

Men are not prisoners of fate, but only prisoners of their own minds.

—Franklin D. Roosevelt

You are about to embark on an adventure (drum roll, please)…into your own mind. In this chapter we'll help you learn to observe your mind. Along the way, you'll learn about its amazing abilities—and its sneaky traps. Not to give the whole thing away, but you'll discover that your thoughts can lead you astray, just like your feelings can. In this chapter we'll focus on observing thoughts. Then, in chapter 8, we'll help you connect your observations to effective action using deciding and doing skills.

Tilting at Windmills

As with feelings, mindful warriors learn to observe their thoughts and not be pushed around by them. To get an idea of how the flip side works—what a mindless battler does—consider a famous character from literature: Don Quixote. He gets so obsessed with books on knights and princesses that he decides to go on a "noble" quest. He puts on an old suit of armor, gives his skinny horse the magnificent new name Rocinante, and rides out into the countryside in search of adventure. His delusions get him in all kinds of trouble: He mistakes a common tavern for a castle and asks the owner to knight him, and then he mistakes a windmill for a giant and battles it.

Don Quixote may be a warrior of sorts, but he isn't what you'd call a mindful warrior. He lives in a world totally romanticized and even invented by his mind. He believes everything that his mind creates. He wastes his time getting into battles that are totally unrelated to real life and only result in him or his sidekick, Sancho Panza, getting beaten up.

Thankfully, most people aren't likely to end up fighting windmills like Don Quixote. But any of us can get caught up in our mind's creations if we aren't careful. The human mind can be tricky because it's smart—very smart. So in this chapter we're going to teach you how to notice its games and not get fooled by the tricks it sometimes plays.

The Mind Is a Problem-Finding Machine

To understand the mind, we find it helpful to think about it like a machine that has a basic operating system and many tasks to perform. Some of these tasks are obvious, like keeping your body alive. There are countless other tasks that are not so obvious. Here are just a few of them:

- Processing a vast amount of information coming at you all at once

- Making sense of all of that information

- Identifying and fixing any problems it finds

- Evaluating how well it's doing (Yes, your mind even examines itself.)

- Evaluating how well you're doing (Though it may seem like that's just the same as evaluating how well your mind is doing, they are different, and that makes things tricky.)

- Comparing how you're doing to how everyone else seems to be doing

We could go on (and on…and on), but you get the idea. To summarize, the mind is a problem-finding and problem-solving machine, and it takes these jobs very seriously. Its job is to locate and fix problems both outside and inside your mind and body. The following table shows how the mind goes about its work with these two kinds of problems.

How the Mind Works			
	Problem finding (*Is there a problem?*)		**Problem solving** (*How do I solve it?*)
Outside your mind and body	*Is that a lion?*	If yes →	*How do I escape it?*
Inside your mind and body	*Are my thoughts painful?*	If yes →	*How do I escape them?*

But as you learned in chapters 5 and 6, there's a huge difference between solving problems in the outside world and solving them inside. You can get rid of the garbage in your house, but you can't really get rid of difficult thoughts and feelings.

Solving problems in the outside world is, of course, extremely useful. It got our species to where we are today. Humans have learned to build bridges to solve the problem of crossing mighty rivers, we've invented phones (and Facebook, Myspace, texting, and Twitter) to solve the problem of communication across great distances. However, solving an inside problem like painful thoughts isn't the same. When the mind tries to solve them, it typically fails because these thoughts are a natural part of us and are connected to things we care about. For example, if you think you'll be terrible at speaking in front of your class, your mind is likely to try to solve this problem for you, perhaps by creating lots of reasons why you shouldn't give a speech. In this way, your mind helps solve the immediate problem of "terrible speech," but that actually doesn't help you if you care about increasing your skill at public speaking. You need to practice to get better at it. Your mind gives you a solution (avoid speaking because you're "terrible" at it), but the solution doesn't work.

To understand how the mind got to be a problem-finding machine, let's backtrack to prehistoric times. Many people think that problem solving helped early humans survive. The mind needed to keep people from being injured or killed by wild animals and other threats. Back then, finding and solving problems was a matter of life and death.

Exercise: Figuring Out Who's for Lunch

Here's a quick quiz to help you see how helpful the mind can be in its role as a problem-finding machine. Let's assume that there's a small band of people—Luis, Gabriella, Isaac, Kaitlyn, Ariana, and Stuart—and that they live in a place where hungry lions are often on the prowl. Now imagine that they see an indistinct brown shape in the distance, half hidden by the grass. Before you take the quiz, we'll let you in on a secret: that indistinct brown shape in the grass *is* a hungry lion.

Now that you have all of that background information, read the descriptions of each person below and then check off whether each is likely to get eaten or not.

Problem	Gets eaten	Doesn't get eaten
Luis's mind is very sensitive to problems. He hides in his cave a lot and is very careful.		
Gabriella is very calm and relaxed, which seems great, but she tends to wander through the grass carelessly.		
Isaac's problem-finding ability is good and he can spot lions when he wants to, but he can turn his problem-finding machine off whenever he feels like it.		
Kaitlyn can't turn off her problem-finding mind. She spends all her time looking for danger.		
Ariana's problem-finding mind is supersensitive. It finds all the lions, but it also tends to think there are lions behind every patch of grass, even when there aren't.		
Stuart's problem-finding mind isn't sensitive enough. His mind fails to notice lions, and he spends a lot of time lost in daydreams.		

The people who get eaten are Gabriella, Isaac, and Stuart. Gabriella doesn't have a very good problem-finding machine. Sadly, she would probably get eaten by the first lion that comes along. Isaac would be fine as long as he doesn't turn off his problem-finding machine. But if he decides to turn it off one day, then he's more likely to get eaten by a lion than is Kaitlyn, who can't turn hers off. As to Ariana, being too sensitive may be a different kind of problem, but she never fails to run from a lion. And because Stuart sometimes doesn't detect problems, he stands a good chance of becoming lunch.

Those answers may seem pretty obvious, but hopefully the quiz did help you understand some key points about your mind as a problem-finding machine:

- *The mind's main job is to make sure you survive by finding problems and solving them.*

- *Because survival is your mind's first priority, it needs to be supersensitive in order to detect the tiniest problem.*

Here's what else you need to know: No one has a mind like Isaac's. You simply can't turn off the problem-finding machine. But there is something you can do. You can observe your mind in action and notice when it's in overdrive. When you notice that your problem-finding mind is in overdrive, you can choose how to respond, instead of buying into what your mind is telling you and reacting without thinking. For example, you can hear your mind saying you're "not good enough" but still do your best.

Thinking about prehistoric humans and the problem-finding machine is all fine and good, but what about now? How does all of this problem finding work out for people in modern times, when most people don't face threats like lions? Let's take a look at Sam's situation to see an example of how it often plays out.

• *Sam: Noticing the Problem-Finding Machine*

I've noticed that since I've been suspended from school, all I do is sit around trying to figure out what's wrong with me. It's like I want to find the part of me that's defective and just destroy it or remove it.

I mean, I feel like I ruined Dorian's life. I spend most of my time trying to figure out how I got it so messed up and feeling sick about it. Everywhere I look, it seems like I'm reminded of what's wrong with me. Even things I used to really like doing remind me of all my problems. When I go to the skate park, if I see other people I think they must be laughing at me, like I laughed at that kid Dorian. And when I think of that hot girl Sandy, I end up hating myself instead of dreaming about her.

My mind runs all day, criticizing me. If I had to name my mind, I'd call it "the Punisher." I can even picture a sign above my head:

Problem-Finding Overdrive

Can you see how Sam's problem-finding machine is working in overdrive? It can't stop trying to find problems. His mind is searching for what's wrong with him, searching for the problem inside his mind and body.

Maybe you've felt that way sometimes too. One way to turn the tables so that your mind works for you, rather than the other way around, is to engage the observing skills of a mindful warrior. That means noticing when your mind machine starts running in overdrive, then naming it when you see it. You can even give your mind a name, like Sam did, and say something to yourself like *Ah, there's "the Punisher," hard at work trying to find problems with me and solve them.*

If that sounds a little weird—or maybe even impossible—don't worry. Observing your mind at work takes practice. No one gets it instantly. So to give you some practice and help you see how clever your mind is about finding problems, here's another exercise.

Exercise: Noticing the Problem Finder

In this exercise, your job is to practice observing. For now, we won't explain the point or what's likely to happen. Just follow the instructions as closely as you can, and let your mind do its job. All you need to do is read the next statement, close your eyes and say the statement quietly to yourself, and then just notice what your mind does. Ready? Here's the statement:

I am a person who is likable.

What did your mind say about this? Did it evaluate the statement as "right" or "wrong"? Perhaps it had thoughts that just argued against the statement or speculated about what the purpose of reading it was. Be patient and read on.

Here's another statement. Once again, read it, close your eyes and say it quietly to yourself, and then notice what your mind does:

I am a person who is lovable.

What did your mind have to say about that statement? Did it criticize or try to troubleshoot the idea?

Keep going by reading the next statement, closing your eyes and saying it quietly to yourself, and once again noticing any thoughts or messages your mind has about the statement:

I am a person who is complete.

How did your mind like that? At this point, you might be ready to find out why we want you to read this. Like we said, the mind is tricky. Don't worry about or try to change what your mind is doing. Remember, your job here is to just observe.

Ready? Here's one final statement for you to read and then say to yourself.

I am perfect.

What did you notice your mind doing this time?

Looking at the mind this way can feel pretty weird at first. Sometimes it's easier to see how someone else's mind approaches this kind of task. So let's look at how Jess did with this exercise. Then we'll explain what it's all about.

• *Jess: Noticing the Problem Finder*

I am a person who is likable.

This is a really stupid exercise. If I were likable, I wouldn't feel like I had to run away all the time. I wonder why anybody thinks it's a good idea for me to read a statement like this. Maybe they want me to believe this about myself. Fat chance!

I am a person who is lovable.

I guess I am loved by some people, but honestly, this is another stupid sentence. If I were lovable, why would my best friend hate me?

I am a person who is complete.

Now that's just silly. I'm not going to my friends' houses or the mall. I run away from anything difficult. My friends hate me. How can I possibly be complete?

I am perfect.

As if that's true! I am definitely not perfect. I always say the wrong thing—or freeze and don't know what to say. If I were perfect, I wouldn't have made such a mess of things.

Problems, Problems, Everywhere

Jess's mind did exactly what we've seen with many people we've worked with. It went straight into trying to figure out whether the statements matched her idea of herself. Yep, that's right: it set to work finding problems with seemingly good things.

How about you? Did you observe your mind having thoughts similar to Jess's?

Most people who do this exercise say they noticed their mind fighting the statements. They notice thoughts like *Oh no, I am definitely not perfect, If I were complete, I wouldn't feel so bad*, or even *What's the point of this stupid exercise, anyway?* If that sounds like you, here's what was happening: Your problem-finding machine was doing its job. It was taking in the information, finding problems with it, trying to solve those problems, and trying to figure out the purpose. Your mind takes this job very seriously.

Here's another question: Did your mind spot any hidden tricks?

Let's look at the instructions for the exercise again: "All you need to do is read the next statement, close your eyes and say the statement quietly to yourself, and then just notice what your mind does." There were no instructions saying that you should believe those statements. We didn't ask you to decide whether you are likable, lovable, complete, or perfect. We just asked you to read each statement and observe how your mind reacted.

What's worth noticing is that the problem-finding machine is always looking for problems—even when there isn't a problem for you or about you. In fact, your mind gets really serious about finding problems that include one of the smallest words in the English language: "I." Your mind does a lot of evaluating and criticizing whenever the word "I" is around.

The Wrap-Up

In this chapter you learned that your mind is a problem-finding machine. Its intentions are good: it wants to help you survive. Because that's an important job, it works really hard to stay in control and figure everything out for you. There are two main parts to its job description:

- **Problem finding:** The mind is always searching for things that might harm you. Sometimes it gets carried away with this job.

- **Problem solving:** The mind tries to fix every problem, and it tends to get carried away with this job too.

The mind can be pretty good at solving problems in the outside world. However, the mind machine isn't so great when it turns your thoughts and feelings into problems to be solved. Sometimes it even turns *you* into a problem and tries to figure out what's wrong with you or why you aren't "good enough."

Your mind is the most powerful thing on the planet. *But*, you're ultimately running the machine. Mindful warrior skills will help you learn about it by observing it in action. And once you can observe it, you can get better at choosing whether or not to listen to it. And the truth is, you don't have to listen to it all the time. Pretty cool, huh?

Chapter 8

not buying the mind's evaluations

BOLD Warrior Skills	
Breathing deeply and slowing down	
Observing	✓
Listening to your values	✓
Deciding on actions and doing them	✓

Most of the important things in the world have been accomplished by people who have kept on trying when there seemed to be no hope at all.

—Dale Carnegie

In the previous chapter you learned to observe your mind and look at it as a machine that does an incredible job of finding problems and trying to solve them. In this chapter we're going to go deeper into the mind and observe it at its trickiest. In particular, we're going to focus on how it always seems to be evaluating things and trying to convince you that its evaluations are correct. The good news is that even though the mind can be tricky sometimes, with practice you can notice this and learn how to act effectively—how to decide on actions and do them—even when your mind is evaluating like crazy.

The Mind Is an Evaluator

As you now know, the mind is always searching for potential problems. There's another important aspect of the mind that you need to know about. It has a lot of opinions about what's "good" and "bad," and it tends to think that you're always right and other people are usually wrong. When the mind really gets going, it generates incredibly convincing messages. The next exercise will help you understand just how persuasive it can be—and how unreliable its evaluations sometimes are.

Exercise: Observing Evaluations

Imagine you meet a girl named Jordan and become friends with her. (If you're a guy, you might find this exercise easier if you imagine your new friend is also a guy.) You like Jordan and you have lots of fun together. You want to spend most of your free time with her. You like the way she talks, the clothes she wears, the books she reads… In fact, there isn't much about Jordan that you don't like. You can't imagine getting angry with Jordan—ever. Look at the friendship meters below and place an X on each line to indicate your answers to the questions.

How friendly does Jordan seem right now?

Friendly $\longleftrightarrow$ Unfriendly

How would you be likely to act toward Jordan?

Friendly $\longleftrightarrow$ Unfriendly

You also have another friend, Alicia, who doesn't like Jordan as much as you do. She starts to say a few critical things about Jordan, like "Have you noticed how annoying her voice is?" and "Did you see how she flirts with the boys?" And then Alicia makes the big statement: "Jordan acts like she is so much cooler than you!" (Again, if you're a guy, you may want to change up this scenario so Jordan is a guy.)

What do you think would happen to how you see Jordan's behavior and your friendship? Rate your feelings again, placing an X on the friendship meters below.

How friendly does Jordan seem after the negative gossip?

Friendly $\longleftrightarrow$ Unfriendly

How might you act toward Jordan now?

Friendly $\longleftrightarrow$ Unfriendly

This is where your mind can get really sneaky. Before you knew it, it probably started evaluating Jordan in negative ways. You might even have started to "see" so many annoying things about Jordan that you wondered how you ever got to be friends at all. But notice that you never had any direct experience of Jordan doing anything wrong. She wasn't mean to you directly. The new perspective on Jordan came from Alicia's thoughts and words, which colored your own thoughts and set your mind to work on figuring out whether Jordan is really as annoying as Alicia thinks and figuring out whether liking Jordan was a mistake.

There's a good chance your mind became so persuasive that it convinced you there are many problems with Jordan. Although your mind saw her as a best friend forever at the beginning, now it sees her as so annoying that you can barely stand to be in the same room.

You see, your mind is always evaluating other people and trying to give you advice about them. Sometimes that advice is helpful. It might allow you to build friendships or steer you clear of people who genuinely aren't good for you. But sometimes it isn't so helpful. For example, it might make you see enemies where there are none.

The Mind Is a Storyteller

Another surprising thing the mind does is weave information into stories—usually stories about you and your life. And because the mind is also an evaluator, often these stories carry a lot of messages about the kind of person you are—messages that aren't necessarily true.

As is often the case, it's easier to see this happening to other people. So in a minute, we'll observe how Jess's mind creates stories about her life. Jess is seventeen years old, which means she's lived for almost 150,000 hours. To help manage the details and make the information usable, her mind tries to condense all of those hours into a short, streamlined story, almost like those sound bites you hear on the news.

To give you an idea of how this works, here are two stories Jess tells about herself. The first is something she said when she introduced herself to her English class at the beginning of the school year. The second is her first entry in a blog she's decided to start. As she says the first one, she's groaning under her breath and thinking, *Another year and another stupid "introduce yourself" session. Ugh.*

• *Jess Introduces Herself to Her English Class*

I'm Jess. I'm seventeen. My two brothers and I live with our mother. I like music. I don't like English class very much, but I do love to read. My favorite books are detective novels and mysteries.

At this point, Jess's mind says, *Oh no! I can't think of anything else to say. I am such a loser. Quick! Sit down!*

• *Jess Starts a Blog*

Dear World,

I guess I should introduce myself. I'm Jess. I'm seventeen. I love music.

I used to have a great life. I used to have great friends. But now I don't have any friends I can trust anymore.

Since I started high school, things just haven't been the same. I loved school before that. I had the same friends for four years. And the teachers were nicer than in high school.

My sixth-grade teacher, Mr. Johnson, was really fun, and he was kind to me too. He must have liked something about me. He always gave me hard math problems, and he thought I was good at them. He also wrote really nice comments in my yearbook.

Now everything is a mess. I don't like going to school, and I've lost my friends. That's the worst part of my life—not having friends and hating the thought of going to school.

Does either of the two stories above capture all of who Jess is? Of course not. Jess has recalled just a few main events, many of them related to the recent past. Her mind has shortened the stories of her life, transforming all of her almost 150,000 hours into bite-size, easily accessed chunks. It doesn't seem to matter whether she's introducing herself to a new class or writing about herself on a blog; her mind "helpfully" gives her an oversimplified account of herself. And because Jess worries a lot, her mind also tries to "help her" by encouraging her to rush through more challenging tasks, like introducing herself in class.

Exercise: Observing Your Own Storytelling Machine

What kind of stories does your mind tell you about yourself? Does it try to describe you in just a few words or sentences, like *I'm fat* or *I'm dumb*?

This kind of condensing of information can be useful for things like summarizing the meaning of Shakespeare or describing the rules of trigonometry. But you can never be described using just a few words. There are billions of pieces of information—experiences, thoughts, feelings, and qualities—that make up the real you.

To help you observe how your mind might be taking shortcuts to define you, take a look at the following list. It includes some common thoughts that the mind tends to throw at people. Check off any evaluations that your mind sometimes offers about you:

☐ *I'm a worthless person.*   ☐ *I'm ugly.*

☐ *I can't stand myself.*   ☐ *I'm a disappointment.*

☐ *I have nothing to be proud of.*   ☐ *I'm disgusting.*

☐ *I'm no good.*   ☐ *I'm broken.*

☐ *No one likes me.*   ☐ *I'm damaged.*

☐ *No one loves me.*   ☐ *There's something wrong with me.*

☐ *I'm an imposter.*   ☐ *I'm useless.*

☐ *There's nothing special about me.*   ☐ *I'm boring.*

☐ *I'm bad.*   ☐ *I'm invisible.*

☐ *I'm not worth it.*   ☐ *I don't belong.*

If you checked a number of these statements, you're in good company. Everybody criticizes themselves with statements like these. Everybody has a problem-finding mind, and it seems the thing our minds love to do the most is evaluate ourselves. The mind likes to look at you just to see whether there's a problem to fix in comparison with how other people are doing. It asks, *Am I good enough? What's wrong with me? Can other people see my flaws?*

Exercise: Evaluating the "Bad" Cup

Here's a weird exercise that will help you notice the difference between you and your mind's stories about you. To do this exercise, you'll need a cup. Any cup from your kitchen will do, but if you have a favorite cup, that's best.

Put the cup in front of you and use your mind to say mean things about it. (We did say this was a weird exercise.)

Use your mind to really beat that cup up. Evaluate the ways in which the cup is bad, useless, ugly, or even stupid. Just take a moment to let your mind evaluate that cup, abuse it, and find everything that's wrong with it.

Now look at the cup again. After all of your abuse, has the cup changed? Or has it stayed exactly the same?

Obviously, it hasn't changed. So no matter what your mind says about it, the cup stays the same.

The same is true for you. The things your mind says about you don't change who you truly are.

The mind is tricky. It will try to convince you that "bad" is in the cup or that "bad" is in you. It will try to convince you that "bad" is something real, like a knife in your stomach.

The tricks your mind plays to persuade you that things are bad are just like this bad cup exercise and the example of Alicia and Jordan. The things your mind evaluates don't change. The cup stayed the same. Jordan stayed the same. What changes is *your view* of things, and sometimes this happens in such a sneaky way that you don't even notice what's going on. If your mind gets overactivated, it can convince you that an angel is a demon and a demon is an angel. It can make your friends seem unfriendly, even though they haven't changed in the least. And it can make you think that you're faulty, even when you haven't made any mistakes.

Never Mind Your Mind

How do you see through the tricks? The key is to practice observing and then deciding what to listen to. If you observe the mind at work, you can catch it in the process of trying to convince you. Observing gives you something really valuable: the power to notice that your mind is doing its job, the power to choose what you will do with those evaluations, and the power to choose whether you need to act on them.

Mindless battlers believe all of their mind's evaluations and follow all of its advice, whether helpful or unhelpful. They don't see that they have a choice. When their minds say, *You can't do it* or *You aren't good enough,* mindless battlers believe this and stop trying to do things—even things that really matter to them.

Mindful warriors learn to slow down, observe the mind machine at work, and be wary of its evaluations. They learn to listen to their values and then make decisions based on what's important to them (We'll talk a lot about values in the later chapters). If they decide the mind's advice will help them get more of what's important to them, then they follow that advice. And when the mind's advice isn't helpful, they simply say to themselves, *Never mind my mind*, in that moment.

Exercise: Learning Not to Mind Your Mind

As we've said, the mind is extremely advanced. So it stands to reason that we tend to think it's infallible. It can be hard to say, "Never mind my mind." To help you get a little practice doing so, look over the following table and decide what you would do in each situation. Read across each row, then, in the right-hand column, circle what you'd choose to do if you listen to your values.

Observing what your mind says	Observing what you do when you listen to your mind	Listening to your values (what you care about)	Deciding what to do
I'm a failure at math.	Give up or do less.	Learning at my own level and doing my personal best	Option 1: Listen to my mind. Give up. Option 2: Never mind my mind.
If I don't punch this kid, I'm a spineless wimp.	Punch someone.	Getting along with people and earning their respect	Option 1: Listen to my mind. Punch. Option 2: Never mind my mind.
I'm unlovable.	Avoid asking someone out.	Developing relationships that matter	Option 1: Listen to my mind. Avoid. Option 2: Never mind my mind.

As always, there are no right or wrong answers. The decision is up to you. But as you might guess, we think that in all of these cases, you'd be better off saying, "Never mind my mind," and choosing to go for what you want.

Choosing Not to Listen to the Mind Machine

A few words of warning: If you choose to never mind your mind, your mind might *really* get going. It might go into hyperdrive in an attempt to, well, change your mind. Don't let this throw you. You can choose to do what's important to you even when the mind machine is going crazy. Don't believe it? Give it a try. Say to yourself, *I can't turn the page of this book.* Repeat it a few times and convince yourself that you really, *really* believe it: *I can't turn the page of this book.* Then turn the page (but then come back to this point and keep reading).

Were you able to turn the page even though your thoughts were saying you couldn't?

Maybe that thought experiment seems a little too simple, so here's another way to think about it. Can you remember times when you did something tough even though your mind doubted you could do it? Did you have doubts and do the thing you wanted anyway? You can feel unmotivated and still act. For example, you can exercise even when you feel tired.

The truth is, you've probably already said, "Never mind my mind," in many situations. Here are some examples:

- Maybe your mind was trying to persuade you to do something mean, like hit or insult someone, but you chose not to.

- Maybe your mind was telling you that you might fail at something, but you went for it anyway.

- Maybe your mind was telling you that you were too tired or bored to do something, but you did it anyway.

One of the most effective ways to "never mind your mind" is to name the kind of thoughts you're having. This is a little strange to describe, but it's very powerful. When you have a difficult thought, try adding one of these two phrases before the thought and then saying it again:

- "I'm having the thought that…"

- "Thank you, Mind, for telling me…"

For example you might say, "I'm having the thought that *I'm a loser*" or "Thank you, Mind, for telling me *I might fail my math class*."

The idea is to rephrase thoughts in a way that helps you begin to notice the machine at work, because you can't turn off your mind—even if sometimes you'd really love to do that. After all, it's a problem-finding machine that runs all the time, and that's mostly a good thing, since it helps you survive. When you "never mind your mind," you get to choose whether or not to act on any given thought. Think of it this way: No thought can make you act inconsistently with your values.

The Wrap-Up

By now, a few things should be clear:

- **The mind is an unreliable advisor.** However, as a mindful warrior, you don't always have to act on every thought it gives you.

- **The mind tells you stories about yourself.** It takes everything that's ever happened to you and condenses it into bite-size chunks. These sound bites aren't the real you. They are words woven into stories.

- **The mind colors the world with its evaluations.** It can change things from good to bad and from bad to good. But often, those things haven't changed; it's just that your mind has persuaded you that they've changed.

- **The mind is convincing.** It puts a lot of effort into making you believe all of the stuff it generates. It wants you to think that its stories and evaluations are 100 percent true and that you should buy into them.

The bottom line? You can't turn your mind off, but you can decide whether or not you must always listen to the advice it gives you.

Chapter 9

developing wise view

BOLD Warrior Skills	
Breathing deeply and slowing down	✓
Observing	✓
Listening to your values	✓
Deciding on actions and doing them	✓

You are what you want to become. Why search anymore? You are a wonderful manifestation. The whole universe has come together to make your existence possible. There is nothing that is not you. The kingdom of God, the Pure Land, nirvana, happiness, and liberation are all you.

—Thich Nhat Hanh

Up to this point, we've been helping you observe the battle within. You've learned to use your breath to anchor yourself in the present moment. You've also learned to be with feelings without battling them and to be with the mind machine without feeling that you have to buy into its stories or that you have to follow its advice. You're almost ready to move on to part 3 of the book, which will help you discover and live the life you want for yourself, using your values to guide you on your journey.

No Limits

Before you begin this journey toward living your values, there's an important question you need to answer: What do you think your limitations are? What do you think you can't do? In part 3 of the book we're going to ask you to think big—to really go for an extraordinary life. But first we have to make sure you aren't going to buy into ideas about your limitations.

Your mind will try to convince you that you can't do certain things. All human minds—yours, ours, your parents'—sometimes generate negative self-evaluations, such as "stupid," "inadequate," "weird," "unlovable," "worthless," "hopeless," "weak," or "unworthy."

What can you do with these kinds of self-limiting thoughts? The first step is to discover *wise view*: a perspective from which you can see your thoughts as passing events, rather than undisputed truths. Wise view is just another observing skill, like the ones you have been practicing throughout this whole book. It gives you a way to get perspective on your life. As you read through this chapter, we'll give you several ways to develop this perspective.

Exercise: Getting a Glimpse of Wise View

Remember how the mind loves to make up stories—and especially stories about you? One problem with stories is that they can lead you to believe that your identity and personality are set in stone and that it's impossible to develop into something else. For example, if you believe a story that says you're unlovable, you'll probably also believe that you'll struggle to find love. If you buy into that story and act as though it were true, it could become a self-fulfilling prophecy.

This exercise will help you see that self-limiting stories are just thoughts that come and go. They aren't permanent, and they don't define you. Like all human beings, you are always changing and evolving. You can choose what to do in each moment and choose who you become. And who you become depends on the things you do in the world.

To help you see that you and your stories about yourself are always changing, in this exercise you'll think back to specific events that happened at different times in your life and even think forward and imagine the future.

About Age Seven

A specific event you remember: _____

_____

_____

What did your body look like? _____

_____

How were you feeling at that time? _____

_____

What were you thinking? _____

_____

_____

About Age Twelve

A specific event you remember: _____

_____

_____

What did your body look like? _____

_____

How were you feeling at that time? _____

_____

What were you thinking? _____

_____

_____

Your Current Age

A specific event that recently happened: _____

_____

_____

What did your body look like? _____

_____

How were you feeling at that time? _____

_____

What were you thinking? _____

_____

_____

About Age Thirty-Five

In this last section, we want you to try to imagine what you might be like when you are thirty-five years old. See if you can just imagine yourself, even though you won't really know what it will be like.

An event that might happen to you: _____

_____

_____

What would your body look like? _____

_____

What might you feel at that time? _____

_____

What might your thoughts be like? _____

_____

_____

Think about these four ages and then answer this question: As you live your life, which part of you remains the same? _____

This seems like a straightforward question, but it's actually really hard, so we'll help you notice what doesn't stay the same.

Body: Your seven-year-old body and thirty-five-year-old body won't be the same.

Feelings: Your feelings as a seven-year-old won't be the same when you're thirty-five. Take sadness, for example. When you're thirty-five, you'll feel an adult kind of sadness, not the sadness of a little kid.

Thoughts: This is easier. You know your thoughts as a thirty-five-year-old definitely won't be those you had when you were seven. You probably won't be saying you want to play in a sandbox!

So, what stays the same, then? It's *you*.

Many things may change, but you are always here. "You" aren't just your body. "You" aren't just your feelings. And "you" aren't just your thoughts. "You" are the observer that knows and sees your body, feelings, and thoughts. This is what we call wise view.

The Observer Within

As you look across the years, you can see that things are always changing. Yet *you* are still there, able to observe everything that changes. It may sound a bit strange, but the one thing that you experience as staying the same is the *you* that learned about your world, the *you* that moved your body, the *you* that did the feeling, and the *you* that did the thinking. And *you* can even imagine what *you* might think and feel in twenty years.

Strange, isn't it? And even though this is true for everyone, everywhere, many people don't take advantage of this ability to stand back and observe themselves. When you get into wise view, you won't be so quick to buy your stories about yourself, especially stories about how you can't do things. It will help you see that there is *you*, and there are stories about you and who you are. With wise view, your core self stays the same even as the stories change.

Sometimes your mind gives you stories about how you are bad, weird, or not good enough. You might feel tempted to believe these stories. For example, you might think, *I really am weird*. The problem-finding mind has a way of focusing your thinking on your limitations. But remember: You can watch these stories unfold, so there is a "you" and there are the stories. You are more than what you think you are.

Exercise: Predicting the Future

To illustrate this idea, look at the picture below and then, in the space below, describe what you think it is. Go on to make up a story about it and write it down. Do this before you read ahead.

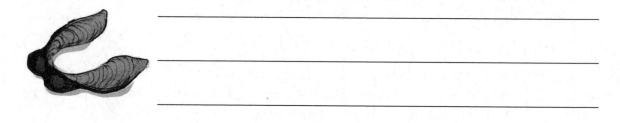

_____

_____

_____

_____

_____

_____

_____

That image was the seed of a maple tree. Now imagine that the seed becomes the tree in the following image.

Think about it. Was there anything in the first image, or in your story, that told you that shape would become a beautiful tree? Maybe you knew it was a maple seed, but for the purposes of this exercise, assume you didn't know that. A maple seed looks nothing like a maple tree. It's small. It's brown. It looks fragile. If you had no knowledge about maple seeds, your mind couldn't look at the seed and figure out that it would become a maple tree. Similarly, your mind cannot look at you and figure out what you will become.

Exercise: Trying On Wise View

Here's another way to experience wise view. In this exercise, you'll rapidly switch between three different types of thinking.

1. First, smile and imagine something really positive—maybe succeeding at something important to you, having fun with a friend, or playing with a pet. Generate some positive thoughts.

2. Next, make an angry face and imagine something that makes you feel mad—like someone treating you or a friend unfairly. Generate some angry thoughts.

3. Finally, make a sad face and imagine something that makes you feel sad—maybe losing someone or something important to you or missing an opportunity to do something you care about. Generate some sad thoughts.

Notice how you changed your thoughts three times, and yet deep down you stayed the same. You were there, silently observing, noticing the changing thoughts and feelings. This is what we mean by wise view.

With wise view, you can watch self-doubting thoughts come and go. You don't have to change them. Getting into wise view is like discovering freedom.

Exercise: Having a Thought vs. Being a Thought

Here's an exercise that will help you practice seeing yourself as separate from your thoughts. Look through the following list of evaluations and check off any thoughts that you sometimes believe about yourself:

☐ Lazy	☐ Unmotivated	☐ Insecure	☐ Obnoxious
☐ Stupid	☐ Ineffective	☐ Defective	☐ Deficient
☐ Worthless	☐ Incompetent	☐ Odd	☐ Disgusting
☐ Weak	☐ Undeserving	☐ Pitiful	☐ Average
☐ Moody	☐ Vulnerable	☐ Ugly	☐ Useless
☐ Unlovable	☐ Bad	☐ Damaged	
☐ Weird	☐ Mean	☐ Inadequate	
☐ Impulsive	☐ Hopeless	☐ Unworthy	

Like most people, you probably had a few things you could check off on that list. Now we are going to show you how to use wise view with these thoughts. In wise view, all we want to do is notice that there is a difference between *having* a thought and *being* a thought. First, take one of the evaluations that you checked off and put it into the following blanks.

1. I am _____.

2. I'm having the thought that I am _____.

3. Using wise view, I see that I *have* thoughts, I do not need to *be* thoughts, and I notice that wise view thoughts seem easier to have.

4. This thought does not have to stop me from doing what's important to me.

Here's an example. See if you notice that when you feel you *are* thoughts (*I am disgusting*), it seems much heavier than when you look at it as *having* thoughts.

1. I am *disgusting*.

2. I'm having the thought that I am *disgusting*.

3. Using wise view, I see that I *have* thoughts, I do not need to *be* thoughts, and I notice that wise view thoughts seem easier to have.

4. This thought does not have to stop me from doing what's important to me.

This is a simple exercise to help you notice that you have thoughts, and you are not the thoughts. You do not need to *be* what you think. After all, you have all sorts of thoughts: good thoughts, ugly thoughts, and unimportant thoughts. Think of yourself as a glass. Sometimes there's an unpleasant beverage in the glass—maybe something bitter, like medicine. Other times there's a tasty beverage in the glass. Either way, the glass doesn't change. Similarly, you hold all of your positive and negative evaluations, along with all of your other thoughts and feelings, both positive and negative. You're the glass, not its contents; the part of you that observes all of this doesn't change.

Wise View and Kindness toward Yourself

The human mind tends to be negative. This is because of the focus on finding problems that has helped our species survive and thrive. Wise view allows you to choose how to act even when the mind is at its most negative. Wise view also gives you the opportunity to do something decidedly positive: practice kindness toward yourself. You can see yourself in a compassionate light, as someone who struggles and suffers and as someone who has the right to hope for love and success.

Many people are afraid of being kind to themselves. They fear that if they act nice toward themselves, they'll lose control or let all of their flaws show.

Exercise: Discovering Whether You're Afraid of Being Kind to Yourself

Read through the following thoughts and check off any that you believe:

☐ *If I'm kind to myself, I'll be weak and lose self-control.*

☐ *If I accept my flaws, I'll become more flawed.*

☐ *Being hard on myself helps me keep my flaws hidden.*

☐ *I don't deserve to be kind to myself.*

☐ *If I don't criticize myself, I'll lose my motivation.*

☐ *If I don't criticize myself, other people won't like me.*

☐ *In order to succeed in life, I've got to be tough on myself.*

If you checked a few of those boxes, you're not alone. Many people fear that being kind to themselves and letting their guard down will cause problems.

However, these beliefs are just plain wrong. The fact is that people who act with kindness toward themselves are actually better at adjusting to stressful situations. They can also be more self-disciplined. This point is worth emphasizing: Self-compassion is often associated with *more* strength, not less.

So what's going on here? Why would self-compassion be associated with strength?

Think about your inner critic as being like a mean teacher. Imagine that teacher calling you all kinds of names and totally disrespecting you. Are you going to work very hard for that teacher? We doubt it. Similarly, when your mind is being unkind to you, it doesn't tend to motivate you to do your best. So, if you can't motivate yourself with meanness and criticism toward yourself, maybe self-compassion is worth a try.

Exercise: Practicing Wise View and Self-Compassion

This exercise can help you use wise view and self-compassion to deal with self-doubt. It builds on earlier exercises and, for the first time in the book, brings all of the BOLD warrior skills together.

To do this exercise, pick one of the self-criticisms you checked off in the exercise "Having a Thought vs. Being a Thought." Choose one that's a bit sticky, by which we mean one that you sometimes believe. Then use that self-criticism in the following process:

1. **Breathe deeply and slow down.** Breathe in (saying, *In, two, three*, to yourself) and out (saying, *Out, two, three*) for a few breaths.

2. **Observe.** "I'm having the thought that I am _____ (insert self-criticism). There is me observing, and me having the thought that I am _____ (self-criticism)."

3. **Listen to your values.** Do you value kindness toward yourself? (Hopefully you do. Everyone deserves self-compassion.) If you do, listen to that value.

4. **Decide how to act with kindness toward yourself and then do it!**

You may wonder how to act with kindness toward yourself. If you aren't sure, start by imagining what you would say to a close friend who was struggling with self-doubt.

What kind words would you say to your friend? Let yourself say those words silently now.

What kind actions might you do to comfort or reassure your friend? Imagine doing those things now.

Now, here comes the hard part. Are you willing to treat yourself as you would your friend? Are you willing to direct this kindness toward yourself?

Thinking about being kind to yourself is a start, but we want you to actually treat yourself with more kindness in day-to-day life. What are some kind words you can say to yourself when you're being hard on yourself?

_____

_____

_____

Likewise, take the time to write down some kind things you can do for yourself when you're being critical of yourself. For example, maybe it would help to chat with a supportive friend, listen to music, take a bubble bath, or do something fun. These activities can help you get out of your mind and into your life.

_____

_____

_____

Let's take a look at how it went for Sam when he did this exercise. But before you read on, we have a question: From what you've learned about Sam, do you think self-compassion will be hard for him?

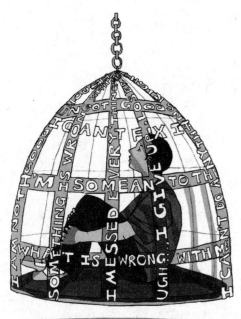

• ## Sam: Trying On Self-Compassion

Since I've started working on observation skills, I've noticed that my mind tends to be full of self-criticism. I'm always saying stuff to myself like I hate myself. I'm mean. I never seem to do anything right. Something is wrong with me, and I can't fix it.

But it feels a little bit different now. I know that this is the problem-finding mind at work. When I listen to what my mind is saying, I realize that I'm really beating myself up. It's good that I'm noticing it.

Usually I'd just act angry to distract myself from how bad I feel about myself. But since that doesn't seem to be working out great, maybe I'll try this weird "wise view" exercise.

1. **Breathe deeply and slow down.** _Okay, I'll take a couple of deep, slow breaths._

2. **Observe.** _"I'm having the thought that_ there is something wrong with me. _I notice that my mind is busy being mean—being "the Punisher."_

3. **Listen to your values.** _Well, really I just want to be at the skate park. So I guess that means I do want to do something nice for myself._

4. **Decide how to act with kindness toward yourself and then do it!** _Okay. I'm going to head to the skate park. And if I notice "the Punisher" at work, I'll just say, "I'm having the thought that something is wrong with me," and then ride my skateboard anyway._

Now I need to think of some other kind things I could do for myself when I'm being self-critical. I'm not really sure, but here are a few things I could try:

Talking with my friends

Playing guitar

Listening to music

Watching TV with my brother

I guess I could also try saying some of those things, like I'm having the thought that... *(and then stick in any mean thought).*

I'm starting to understand that it isn't about making the thoughts disappear. It's about noticing when I'm stuck in my mind, getting unstuck with BOLD skills, and doing things I care about.

Exercise: Writing a Kind Letter to Yourself

Here's one last way to practice self-compassion. It may sound a little odd, but go ahead and do it—right now. Try approaching yourself with self-compassion so you can see what it feels like.

This is sort of similar to the previous exercise. Start by thinking about what you'd say to a close friend who was really struggling and being self-critical. How would you express kindness to your friend? Then write a letter to yourself and say those things to yourself—the same things you'd say to that friend. Be kind and gentle. Write whatever feels natural and right to you, but one thing you might consider doing is telling yourself that everybody has self-criticism and that it's normal. After all, you don't want to start criticizing yourself for being self-critical!

Dear (your name) _____,

_____

_____

_____

_____

_____

_____

_____

The Wrap-Up

Inadequate, weak, worthless, stupid—these and countless other self-criticisms are evaluations that come and go like the weather. You are like the sky that holds all of the weather. Sometimes the weather is bright and sunny; other times it's dark and gloomy. You need not let the mind machine's evaluations limit you. Even when your mind is trying to beat you up, you can still have fun. You can still choose to listen to your values and do what matters to you.

A good place to start is choosing to be kind to yourself when you're feeling self-doubt. When you observe that you're being unkind to yourself, take a few deep breaths and say something like "My mind is telling me that I'm _____ (negative evaluation). I can observe my mind. Wise view is learning that I can watch my thoughts pass. I can listen to them when they help me, and I can let them go when they don't help me. Even when my mind is tormenting me, I can find ways to be kind to myself."

Part 3

Living Your Way

To the question of your life, you are the only answer. To the problems of your life, you are the only solution.

—Jo Coudert

Chapter 10

knowing what you value

BOLD Warrior Skills	
Breathing deeply and slowing down	
Observing	
Listening to your values	✓
Deciding on actions and doing them	

This above all: to thine own self be true,
And it must follow, as the night the day,
Thou canst not then be false to any man.

—Shakespeare

"Listening to your values." What does that even mean? It probably sounds sort of odd. How do you even discover what your values are? If you feel a bit at a loss, don't worry—that's what this part of the book is all about. In this chapter and the next three, we'll help you figure out what your values are. We'll also help you start to decide on—and do—actions that support your values.

All you need for this kind of adventure is an open heart and mind, along with a willingness to dream, explore, and discover.

Ready? Let's start with a game.

Exercise: Living by the Numbers

Pick six numbers between 1 and 10. You can choose the same number more than once, like 1, 3, 3, 7, 4, 4. No cheating! Don't look ahead to see what this is for.

Write your six numbers here: _____ _____ _____ _____ _____ _____

Now you can read on.

Okay, now with those six numbers, you are about to play the game of life. Your destiny is on the board shown below.

Start at the beginning. First, move the number of spaces indicated by your first number. Then move the number of spaces indicated by your second number, and so on, for six turns. Follow the numbers on the game board to see where you end up—how your life turns out.

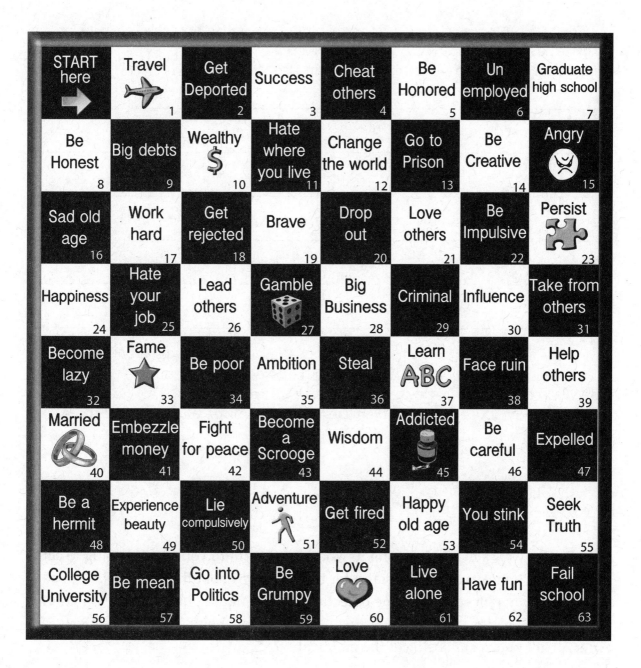

START here →	Travel 1	Get Deported 2	Success 3	Cheat others 4	Be Honored 5	Un employed 6	Graduate high school 7
Be Honest 8	Big debts 9	Wealthy $ 10	Hate where you live 11	Change the world 12	Go to Prison 13	Be Creative 14	Angry 15
Sad old age 16	Work hard 17	Get rejected 18	Brave 19	Drop out 20	Love others 21	Be Impulsive 22	Persist 23
Happiness 24	Hate your job 25	Lead others 26	Gamble 27	Big Business 28	Criminal 29	Influence 30	Take from others 31
Become lazy 32	Fame 33	Be poor 34	Ambition 35	Steal 36	Learn ABC 37	Face ruin 38	Help others 39
Married 40	Embezzle money 41	Fight for peace 42	Become a Scrooge 43	Wisdom 44	Addicted 45	Be careful 46	Expelled 47
Be a hermit 48	Experience beauty 49	Lie compulsively 50	Adventure 51	Get fired 52	Happy old age 53	You stink 54	Seek Truth 55
College University 56	Be mean 57	Go into Politics 58	Be Grumpy 59	Love 60	Live alone 61	Have fun 62	Fail school 63

How did it go? Did you end up rich or in ruins? Did you find love or become a hermit?

Would you have preferred to have some choice in your life? Really? You mean you didn't like having prison or bravery randomly chosen for you?

Okay. So now you can play the game again, but this time you get to choose the six things from the game board that you absolutely want to have in your life.

Write your six choices here (we'll come back to them later in the chapter):

1. _____

2. _____

3. _____

4. _____

5. _____

6. _____

For now, just think about how a lot of people go through life without giving serious thought to what matters to them. Crazy, isn't it—living as though life were just a roll of the dice? People do this for various reasons, but mostly because their minds tell them that choosing is scary. So they just don't choose. Given that you've read this far, we're pretty sure that isn't how you want to live your life.

Living Your Values

Living your values means listening to what's important to you and choosing to act accordingly. It means saying, "I stand for this," "I care about this," or "I want to be about doing this." It can take some detective work to figure out what really matters to you and some courage to put your values into action, but it's worth the effort. After all, it's better than being at the mercy of the dice.

We think a lot of people never realize that they get to choose how to decide on actions that reflect their values. And, of course, a lot of teenagers complain that the adults in their lives don't let them choose. That isn't what you'll get from us. We want you to know that you *do* have choices, and we want to help you explore them. That's the only way you can figure out what living your values means for you—just for you, not for your parents, your teachers, or your friends.

That probably sounds pretty good. But we have to warn you about a few things: Thinking about choices can bring up a lot of uncomfortable feelings. Plus, the mind has a tendency to go into overdrive and start evaluating how you aren't doing enough in your life or how you aren't good enough to have friendship or love. And at this point in the book, you have learned what happens when all those evaluations start coming up in your mind. It can get pretty unpleasant. So be sure to put your mindful warrior skills to work. Notice that thinking about important issues often feels uncomfortable. That's when you need to be especially willing to use BOLD skills and keep following the path that matters to you.

Exercise: Getting a Glimpse of Values

In this exercise, you'll get some practice in deciding on actions in some imaginary situations. It's sort of like a workout in choosing your values. Since it's imaginary, we're giving you some pretty wild scenarios. Write as many answers to each question as you'd like. If you need more space, you can use a separate piece of paper or your journal.

What would you do if you had more money than you could possibly spend?

1. _____

_____

2. _____

_____

3. _____

_____

4. _____

_____

5. _____

_____

6. _____

_____

It would be fun, wouldn't it? If you're like most people, you may have imagined yourself in a fancy house with a pool, owning several expensive cars, going to all the best restaurants, traveling the world, and basically having everything you could possibly desire. Great!

Now imagine that you've bought everything you wanted, traveled the world, had some adventures, and maybe even bought an island. Who knows? Maybe you're even a little bit sick of buying things. What would you do with your life next? For example, maybe you'd work to help other teenagers in need, do something creative, or spend a lot of time with family members, friends, or loved ones. Write your ideas about what you'd do here, and use a separate piece of paper or your journal if you need more space:

1. _____

_____

2. _____

_____

3. _____

_____

4. _____

_____

5. _____

_____

6. _____

_____

    Now look over your answers to those two questions. Does it maybe seem like being rich would be great, but what you do with your life matters even more than what you own?

    Your answers to the second question, about what you'd do after you get tired of spending money, go a long way toward revealing what you value. Why did you choose the things you listed in response to the second question? We hope the answer is because they mean something to you—because they're important and have a great deal of value for you.

Daring to Dream

Civil rights leader Martin Luther King Jr. once said, "If you lose hope, somehow you lose the vitality that keeps life moving, you lose that courage to be, that quality that helps you go on in spite of it all. And so today I still have a dream." We think most people—you included—have a lot in common with Martin Luther King Jr. Most people have big dreams. The key is to think about them and use them to guide your life's course, almost like a compass pointing you in the direction that matters in your life. Here's an exercise to help you do just that.

Exercise: Daring to Dream

Imagine that someone is standing in front of you—someone who really cares about you and wants to know what's important to you. Imagine that this person is intensely interested in your opinions. Answer the following questions as though you were speaking to that person. Don't hold back. This is your chance to share your thoughts with someone who really wants to listen!

    As you answer, watch out for your mind giving you bad advice. For example, it might say that you can't achieve your biggest dreams. The mind is almost always critical when people dare to dream. Just observe this and dare to dream anyway. Also think back and consider the six choices you made in the game of life. Playing with them can help you think of what matters here too.

If you had a magic wand and could change something about the world, what would you change? Jot down the first three ideas you think of:

1. _____

_____

2. _____

_____

3. _____

_____

Choose the idea you like the most and write it here:

_____

Now think about this: What qualities are important in a good friendship? Once again, jot down the first three things that pop into your head:

1. _____

2. _____

3. _____

Now seriously consider what you think the most important quality in a friend is and write it here:

_____

Finally, if you were given a chance to achieve something amazing with your life, what would you choose to do? Don't hold back; there are no limits here! Since this is an exercise in dreaming, write down as many amazing things as you like. If you need more space, use a separate piece of paper or your journal.

1. _____

_____

2. _____

_____

3. _____

_____

4. _____

_____

5. _____

_____

6. _____

_____

How did it go? It takes a lot of courage to even think about these questions. We're guessing that your mind had a lot to say. It can feel scary or wrong to boldly write something like "I'd like to create more love in the world," "I'd like to be a good friend who listens," or "I want to be a best-selling author." Maybe your mind offered some evaluations, perhaps with thoughts like *This exercise is silly.* Or maybe it tried to convince you that you're just not up to realizing your dreams, focusing on limitations and saying things like *I could never do that because…* This may not be fun, but as you now know, it's normal. Whatever thoughts you had are fine. Remember, you can always call on wise view and simply watch them pass.

You may not think any of your dreams are realistic or possible for you. That's okay. A lot of the teenagers we've met think the same thing, and we used to think that way too. Jess definitely does. Let's take a look at what happened when she did this exercise—and how she used BOLD warrior skills to work with her mind's resistance.

• *Jess: Daring to Dream*

What would I do if I had a magic wand and could change something about the world?

1. **I'd stop pollution.**

2. **I'd make people nicer to each other.**

3. **I'd end poverty.**

Out of these ideas, the one I like best is **stopping pollution***.*

As to what qualities are important in a good friendship, I definitely learned a few things about that back when my former best friend, Sally, started spreading rumors about Josh and me. Here are my three ideas:

1. **Being able to trust each other**

2. **Being able to have fun and laugh together**

3. **Doing nice things for each other, like helping with homework**

Out of these qualities, the one that seems most important is being able to trust each other.

Even though it might not seem like it now, I actually have a lot of ideas about amazing things I'd like to do in life (if I had a magic wand, that is):

1. **Be a chef with my own restaurant**

2. **Find the love of my life and share amazing times**

3. **Travel the world, experiencing new cultures and having adventures**

4. **Learn about food from all over the world and then share my passion with friends**

5. **Protest about pollution and help politicians hear how much people care about this**

6. **Eat well and exercise so I look amazingly hot**

7. **Have a family (Wow, that is weird! But I want to do that some day.)**

But even as I write that list, I can hear my mind at work, telling me that I'm pretty dumb to think I can do any of these things. After all, I'm just a teenage loser with no friends and no life. Me, a chef—ha! I'll probably end up working in a factory chopping heads off fish all day. In fact, I'll be lucky if anyone ever hires me, so I should just be satisfied with a boring, dead-end job, if I can even get one.

You know, when I do the mindful warrior thing, I can notice my mind is really working overtime here. I guess that makes it a good time to try some BOLD skills. I'll start by just breathing deeply and noticing what my mind is saying.

The next thing is to observe. I can see problem finding (I'm dumb; I'm a loser) and I can see my mind trying to convince me (I should be satisfied with a dead-end job). Okay, not bad observations, I guess.

Since I really can't run from my mind machine (I wouldn't get far, LOL!), I'll just observe the thoughts and add that saying at the front so I can observe them even better. Here goes:

I'm having the thought that I've ruined my life.

I'm having the thought that nothing good will ever happen to me.

I'm having the thought that I deserve a boring, dead-end job and a boring, dead-end life.

*I'm having the thought that…*Wow! my mind does this negative stuff all the time!

I guess I'm noticing that wise view thing. I am not my evaluations!

Now I need to listen to what I care about—my values. Okay, so my value is to have a future with a career like being a chef and to have friends right now. That's it for now.

The last part of BOLD is to decide on actions and then take them. So my decision is to practice mindful warrior skills and get into wise view, where I can see that I am not my evaluations. And I've also decided to keep being willing to dream, even if I'm really scared.

The Wrap-Up

Learning to live your values is about being willing to dream and discover. Sure, you have to act on them, but the starting place is thinking about your dreams, even if you feel uncertain or scared.

Now that you have an idea of what we mean by listening to your values, the next couple of chapters will help you zero in on what's important to you and help you do more of that every day. After all, living isn't dreaming. Living is doing.

Your problem-finding mind will probably try to discourage you from dreaming. It will tell you that your dreams can't happen—that they're too big or too grand. We don't guarantee that you can achieve your dreams. But one thing is for sure: they're not likely to happen if you don't know what they are. Daring to have big dreams is one of the best ways to discover what you love, what you care about, and what you want to stand for.

Chapter 11

learning to value yourself

BOLD Warrior Skills	
Breathing deeply and slowing down	
Observing	✓
Listening to your values	✓
Deciding on actions and doing them	✓

The journey between what you once were and who you are now becoming is where the dance of life really takes place.

—Barbara DeAngelis

We are all travelers, and each of us could take many possible paths. Which way will you go? We believe the most rewarding path is in the direction of what you value or care about. This chapter (and the next two) will build on what you learned about your values in chapter 10.

Once you know what you care about, you can place your energy and courage in those directions. Your values will help keep you focused and strong, making it difficult for people to knock you off your path for very long. The reverse is also true: If you don't know what you value, you're likely to wander aimlessly or easily get pushed around by others and what they want.

This chapter focuses on helping you identify your values in regard to how you want to develop yourself. It may sound kind of strange, but we'll call them self values. Learning more about your self values can help you work on yourself, and you'll probably notice that understanding and acting on your self values helps you get more enjoyment and satisfaction out of life. Chapter 12 will help you clarify your values in friendships, and chapter 13 will help you clarify your values in regard to the wider world.

Exercise: Clarifying Self Values

Look at the table below, which shows some of the values people often say are important in regard to themselves. These are qualities you might want to have or increase within yourself and in your life. Then, using a scale of 0 to 10, where 0 is not at all important and 10 is of the greatest importance, rate how important each one is to you right now. We've included a few blank spaces where you can fill in any other self values that are especially important to you.

0	1	2	3	4	5	6	7	8	9	10
Not important					Moderately important					Of the greatest importance

Importance	Value	Importance	Value
	Having courage		Learning
	Being creative		Being self-disciplined
	Being wise		Having fun
	Adventuring		Being spiritual
	Being curious		Being attractive
	Enjoying food		Relaxing
	Enjoying entertainment		Being healthy

Once you've rated all of these potential values, take some time to think about the three that you gave the highest ratings. Then think about how you would live by these values. If you were deciding on and doing actions based on those values, what would you be doing? It's best to start with small things. For example, if you value having fun, you might write something like "Having fun matters to me, and I want to notice all the small ways that fun can happen every day, like when you start laughing because a friend is laughing, even though you don't know what's so funny. I want to notice those times."

One important note: Make sure you write about the actions you want to take right now, at this stage of your life. Your values will change in the future, as you change. That's natural. But your current values and goals should reflect who you are right now. Also, really focus on *your* values and not what others might value or think you should value.

In the space below, describe what it would look like to be acting on those top three self values in your life right now:

1. _____

_____

2. _____

_____

3. _____

_____

• Jess: Clarifying Self Values

Thinking about self values was hard. I noticed that I needed to use mindful warrior skills to even think about it. At first my mind was racing, so I took a few minutes to breathe deeply and slow down. I noticed that my mind was saying all sorts of mean things, like Since you're a coward, how can courage be important to you? *Then a cool thing happened: I noticed my mind's evaluations and just thought,* I see you, mind machine, *and started the values exercise anyway, even though I felt scared.*

My top three self values for right now are having courage, learning, and being attractive. As for how they'd look if I were living that way right now, here goes:

1. **Being courageous matters to me, and right now that would mean calling a friend, commenting on a friend's Facebook post, or going to the mall instead of hiding in my room.**

2. **Learning matters to me, and even though I've been doing this by reading and surfing the Net, I want to do more. I'm really interested in cooking, so I could check out different cookbooks online and experiment with exotic cooking.**

3. **Being attractive matters to me. Ever since Sally spread those rumors about me, I've been trying to disappear—wearing boring clothes and just trying to blend in. Living this value would mean starting to do my hair and dress up again. It would also mean noticing when my evaluating mind says I don't look good and letting those evaluations go without trying to make them disappear (even though I really want them to!).**

Exercise: Writing Your Future

It's time to do some more imagining. In this exercise, you'll fast-forward to five years from now and write a short story about what happened to you during those five years. Really try to apply all of your creative, free-thinking skills and don't hold back! This exercise may seem a little like make-believe—or maybe even a little like writing an essay for English class—but it's worthwhile work. And even if this seems like pretend, history shows that to do something, you have to think about it first.

Here are some guidelines for writing your story:

1. Imagine that it's five years from now.

2. Imagine that you've acted on your top three self values.

3. As part of your story, include three successes or satisfying experiences that occurred along the way.

4. Also include two things that went wrong—things that were obstacles or barriers and got in your way.

By the way, if you need some help getting started on your story, you can look ahead to see what Jess wrote when she did this exercise. And as always, if you need more space, you can use a separate piece of paper or your journal.

What did you discover as you dreamed about what your life could be like five years from now? Read over your story and underline the failures and the satisfying experiences. What strategies helped you travel in the direction of your values? What strategies helped you overcome barriers and obstacles?

• *Jess: Writing My Future*

Hi, I'm Jess. I'm twenty-two. Wow, I made it!

I cannot believe how dumb we all were in high school. It wasn't just me. My friends tell me now about all the dumb things they were thinking and doing too. I wish I had known it wasn't just me back then!

As much as I cared about learning even back in high school, I spent most of my time hiding out from my former friends. I was trying to be invisible, and that pretty much kept me from getting very involved in classes. I wanted to be anywhere except school, so one day I got up the courage to ask a neighbor who worked at the local supermarket if there were openings for part-time work in the afternoons, after school. To tell the truth, I was terrified about asking her, but I just kept telling myself that she could only say yes or no and that she probably wouldn't chase after me with a stick or anything crazy like that. She said yes! I started working as a stocker, and it was good to have the money, which I mostly used to buy nice clothes.

I got so bummed out by how things went in high school that I decided not to go to college and just worked at the store full-time. That was cool for a while, because I was learning about what it was like to have a job. It wasn't rocket science, but I had to be reliable, work hard, and learn how to do new things. I gradually started working more and more.

After that, I got super-excited about the idea of being a chef, so I applied for part-time jobs at local restaurants. I applied at about twenty different places. At first I said I wanted to work in the kitchen, but eventually I said I'd do anything: bus tables, mop floors, whatever. I started feeling like I must be the biggest loser ever because no one would even hire me to mop floors. For a while I quit trying.

I kept on experimenting with my cooking and everyone loved what I made, which helped me continue to dream of cooking professionally and sharing my passion for interesting food with other people. Eventually I started looking for restaurant work again and finally got hired. It was like at the store: I had to start small, just doing some basic prep work. But then I got to start making sandwiches and salads. After a year there, I finally worked up the nerve to tell the chef about some menu ideas, and he liked them. He actually used one of them!

Want to hear my grand plan? This fall I'm going to enroll in some basic business classes at the local community college. I'm also going to start saving money so I can eventually go to culinary school.

Oh, and I almost forgot one of the best things! I have a boyfriend who really respects me—and who thinks I'm beautiful!

Don't Give Up on Your Dreams

As you were reading Jess's story, you might have noticed that she started by taking baby steps. Some paid off and led to success, like asking her neighbor about a job. Other steps left her feeling a failure, like not getting a job after so many tries. The important thing is that she kept returning to her values, learning new skills and finding the courage to pursue her dreams.

Distinguishing between Values and Goals

We've spent a fair amount of time helping you figure out your self values. Now we'll spend a little time helping you understand the differences between values and goals—and helping you use them to step forward.

Think of following your values as using a compass to travel west. When exactly would you arrive at "west"? Never! As long as the world is round, you can keep traveling in a westerly direction. Living your values is similar. Here are three important qualities of valued living to keep in mind:

1. Because your values reflect how you'd ideally choose to live, you can never complete them. There's always more life to live and more choices to make about living. For example, if you value living an adventurous life, you never actually arrive at that place; you continue to choose whether or not to embark on adventures.

2. Failure and missteps don't cancel out your values. Even if you don't choose to act on being adventurous today, it doesn't invalidate your love of adventure. Nothing and no one can take your values away from you.

3. Your values are entirely up to you. You may feel like you need to have good reasons for holding certain values, or you may feel that you should have certain values because society or other people think you should. But in the end, values are personal and need to reflect what's important to *you*.

Here's another key point: Listening to and living your values is different from achieving goals. Goals involve concrete actions, things you can check off on a to-do list. Continuing with the example of being adventurous, that's a value—a direction to travel in. Goals are almost like stepping-stones along the way. Concrete goals that might serve your value of being adventurous would be things like going on a backpacking trip or going on a challenging mountain bike ride.

Here's a quick suggestion about setting goals: You're more likely to achieve your goals if they're specific, if you write them down, and if you set a particular time frame for accomplishing them. So in our example, you might write that your goal is to go backpacking in Italy next summer, or you might make a note on your calendar that you're going to ride a certain trail at a certain time the next day.

Exercise: Setting Goals

This exercise will give you some practice in setting goals. Start by selecting a value from this chapter that you'd like to act on more often. It's a good idea to choose a value that's very important to you—perhaps one of the three you selected as most important earlier in the chapter.

Your value: _____

Now ask yourself, *How would I know if I was living my value?* List three specific goals and when you plan to do them. Remember, even baby steps are steps forward:

1. _____

_____

When you'll do it: _____

2. _____

_____

When you'll do it: _____

3. _____

_____

When you'll do it: _____

The Wrap-Up

When you stop to think about it, doesn't it seem bizarre that we have to *plan* to do the things we care about—especially things that are fulfilling for us? Shouldn't we just do this naturally? The truth is, there are a lot of reasons why we don't do what we care about. Sometimes people think they don't deserve to treat themselves well. Sometimes people think self-kindness is a sign of weakness or lack of self-discipline. And a lot of the time, people get so caught up in trying to "succeed" or impress others that they forget to take care of themselves and have fun along the way.

Remember the distinction between values and goals. Values are your compass. They tell you which direction you want to travel in and can't be canceled out by failure, any more than west is canceled out if you accidentally travel east. Goals are concrete things that you can do now. They let you know that you're living according to your values.

Chapter 12

creating friendship

BOLD Warrior Skills	
Breathing deeply and slowing down	✓
Observing	✓
Listening to your values	✓
Deciding on actions and doing them	✓

The only way to have a friend is to be one.

—Ralph Waldo Emerson

Everyone wants to have friends and be liked. Building friendship is about finding people who share your interests and are fun to be around. Even though that might sound easy, you may have discovered that friendship is actually quite complicated. Friendships are constantly changing and evolving. This is especially common with teenagers, who are growing and changing pretty rapidly. Teen friendships often change from one school year to the next, and it isn't unusual for teens to have a best friend for just six months. So during high school and even college, we need to learn a lot about making friends—and a lot about losing friends too. The truth is, we keep learning about friendship throughout life.

What we believe about friendships can influence how we handle changes and challenges in friendships. Do you believe that good relationships should just happen without much effort? Should friends enjoy each other's company all the time? Should love be like a powerful wave that's beyond your control and sweeps you away?

If you answered yes to those questions, you believe that good relationships just happen. While that may be the case sometimes, it isn't the whole truth. We all need to work at making and keeping friends.

This chapter will show you that you don't have to wait around for friendships to happen to you. You can make them more likely to happen, and you can do things to make your current friendships even better. The process starts with figuring out what's important to you in relationships. To help you do that, we'll begin this chapter with an exercise.

Exercise: Understanding What Creates True Friendship

When you're trying to understand what makes for a good friendship, you might be tempted to look at people who are popular. They seem to have a lot of friends, right? Let's go ahead and look at two popular people. Then we'll ask you to decide whether you would want to be friends with them.

Juanita is beautiful and has lots of friends. She talks to everyone—and about everyone. You don't want to get on the wrong side of her because she can be really gossipy. Everyone knows that it's best to act nice to her. It's like she gets to decide who's cool and who isn't.

Based on what you know about Juanita, check the statement that best reflects how you'd feel about being friends with her:

☐ *I probably wouldn't want to be her friend.*

☐ *I feel neutral toward her. Maybe I'd be friends with her and maybe not.*

☐ *I probably would want to be friends with her.*

Tom is great at sports, especially football. Most of the girls think he's sexy, and Tom even says he's hot. There are rumors that he often has a couple of girlfriends at the same time. Tom also gets into fights pretty often, and he usually wins. Nobody messes with him.

Based on what you know about Tom, check the statement that best reflects how you'd feel about being friends with him:

☐ *I probably wouldn't want to be his friend.*

☐ *I feel neutral toward him. Maybe I'd be friends with him and maybe not.*

☐ *I probably would want to be friends with him.*

The teens in these scenarios are popular because they have status or power. Did you want to be their friend? If you said you didn't, you're not alone. People who are popular aren't always well liked. Sometimes they can be mean. They may bully or tease, or they may spread rumors that aren't even true. They may use humor to make fun of others. They may make people feel afraid of being left out. And they may try to control who is included or excluded from the popular group.

Are these the kinds of behaviors you'd want to see a friend engaging in? Is this how you'd want to act toward others? And if these kinds of behaviors don't set the stage for close, genuine relationships, what does?

Exercise: Figuring Out What Matters in Friendships

In this exercise we'll ask you to think about the behaviors you'd like to see in your friends. In the list of behaviors below, check off the five that you most want to see in your friends:

- ☐ Going to parties
- ☐ Being able to see things from your perspective
- ☐ Gossiping
- ☐ Liking the same music as you
- ☐ Letting you be yourself
- ☐ Saying funny things
- ☐ Being kind
- ☐ Being bitchy
- ☐ Sharing stuff
- ☐ Wearing the latest fashions

- ☐ Forgiving your mistakes
- ☐ Enjoying the same activities as you
- ☐ Being a good listener
- ☐ Being good at sports
- ☐ Being curious about things
- ☐ Being loud
- ☐ Acting cool
- ☐ Being honest
- ☐ Being fun
- ☐ Teasing others

The kind of behavior you want to see in your friends is typically the kind of behavior you'll need to engage in to attract those kinds of friends. For example, to have friends who let you be yourself, you need to practice letting other people be themselves. If you want people to really listen to you, you need to practice truly listening to them. This isn't always easy, and as you start to work on this you'll make some mistakes. That's okay. What matters is that you discover your values in regard to friendships and then choose actions that reflect those values.

Exercise: Clarifying Your Values in Relationships

Now it's time to explore the qualities you like to have in friendships and how you like to act toward others. Look at the list below, which shows some of the values that people often say are important in relationships. As you read through the list, think about how you want to be toward others. The focus of this chapter is on friendships, but you can also think about how you'd like to behave in relation to your family and loved ones.

Using the same scale of 0 to 10, where 0 is not at all important and 10 is of the greatest importance, rate how important each value is to you right now, at this point in your life. We've included a few blank spaces where you can fill in any other relationship values that are especially important to you.

0	1	2	3	4	5	6	7	8	9	10
Not important					Moderately important					Of the greatest importance

Importance	Value	Importance	Value
	Understanding others		Forgiving
	Being humble		Communicating well
	Being kind		Being loving
	Being honest		Being accepting
	Being humorous		Being supportive

Now take some time to think about the three that you gave the highest ratings. If you were deciding on and doing actions based on those values, what would you be doing? For example, if being kind is one of your top three values, you might write something like "Kindness is important to me. Whenever I walk into my first class, I want to smile at others and say hello, especially to students I don't know very well." Also, don't forget that values are about what's truly important to you, not what you think is "right" or what you think others would want you to value.

In the space below, describe what it would look like to be acting on those top three values in your life right now:

1. _____

_____

2. _____

_____

3. _____

_____

Inside-Outside Vision

Relationships can be complex and confusing. One minute you may feel like you have a best friend, and the next minute that person isn't speaking to you. What can you do to give yourself the best chance at lasting relationships?

In this section, we'll teach you a new mindful warrior skill, one that strengthens your observing muscles: inside-outside vision. This skill will help you develop and strengthen relationships.

Inside-outside vision actually involves several different skills. When applied to yourself, inside vision is looking at all of the things going on inside you, like thoughts and feelings. Outside vision is looking at what's going on in the outside world, the world outside your body.

Other people are out there in the world outside of you, so you might assume that what you see (outside vision) is what the other person is feeling inside. By now, though, you know that assumptions can be wrong. People are much more complex than they appear. You can look cool on the outside and feel insecure on the inside. Or you can feel sad but put on a happy face. To really understand a person, you have to think about what's going on inside them. That all sounds a little vague, so let's

take a look at an example of how inside-outside vision can be used to build friendships.

Remember Jess's story from chapter 3? She was talking to Josh at a party—just talking, nothing more. But then her best friend, Sally, who had a crush on Josh, saw them talking. Sally got angry and sent Jess a mean text message accusing her of stealing Josh. Jess got worried because Sally was so popular—and such a gossip. The next day when Jess got to school, she saw Sally chatting with a group of girls. Jess started freaking out and thinking, *Why do things always go wrong for me? I've lost all my friends. This is horrible.* She began to isolate herself from her friends, and things really went downhill from there.

But let's examine this situation and see how Jess might have used inside-outside vision when she walked past Sally and that group of girls. Basically, inside-outside vision involves asking yourself four questions along the lines of those in the table below.

	Jess	Sally
Jess's inside vision	**How do I think and feel?** *I feel scared and a little bit angry. I think everyone is talking about me and also think I'll lose all my friends.*	**If I were Sally, how would I feel?** *I can never really know, but if I were Sally, I would feel angry and maybe jealous, and I might also feel pretty insecure.*
Jess's outside vision	**How do I look on the outside?** *I'm trying to look normal and just walk casually past.*	**How does Sally look on the outside?** *She looks cool, like she doesn't care about anything.*

That's inside-outside vision. Notice how different Jess looks on the outside compared to how she's feeling inside. Also notice that Jess can see only the outside of Sally, and what she sees is Sally "acting cool." But when Jess uses her mindful skills and imagines herself in Sally's shoes, she can start to guess that Sally might be feeling differently than how she looks outside.

Do you tend to put on a cool front when you're hurting inside, or do you know people who do this? If you've ever hidden your feelings from others (and we bet you have, because it's pretty common), you can be sure that other people sometimes hide their feelings too.

Exercise: Developing Inside-Outside Vision

Imagining what other people might be feeling inside is a tricky skill. To help you get better at it, here's a two-step process for practicing this skill:

1. **Let go of judgments about yourself and the other person.** Observe your mind and notice whether it's telling stories about you, maybe about how others have hurt you or how you have been misunderstood. Also look for stories about others, maybe about how they were deliberately mean or out to get you. Observe all that storytelling. Does listening to those stories help you? For example, did it help Jess to believe her story that everybody hated her? If the story isn't helping you, simply thank your mind for generating it and then do what's important to you anyway, even if the story says you can't or shouldn't.

2. **Imagine a time when you were in a similar situation.** The best way to guess what someone else is feeling is to remember a time when you were in a similar situation. Once you have that situation in mind, remember everything that was happening: who was there, what everyone said and did, and everything you saw and heard. Use this experience of a similar situation and any pain you felt or challenges you faced to help you imagine what the other person might be feeling.

To give you some practice using these two steps, we'll ask you to imagine when you felt loneliness, fear, and insecurity:

- **Inside:** Think of a time when you were lonely. Imagine that situation vividly and feel the feeling again now. What does it feel like? Where do you feel the loneliness in your body? In your stomach? In your head? All over? Now think of someone in your life who might feel lonely too. Can you imagine how this person's feelings are similar to yours?

- **Inside:** Think of a time when you felt afraid of someone. Imagine that situation vividly and feel the feeling again now. Where do you feel that fear? In your chest? In your stomach? What were you thinking? Now think of someone you know who's afraid of someone else, maybe someone who's getting picked on at school. How might that person feel inside?

- **Inside:** Think of a time you felt insecure, maybe about your looks or your ability at something. Imagine that situation vividly and feel the feeling again now. Where in your body do you feel your insecurity? In your head? In your stomach? Now think of someone you know who might feel insecure too. Can you imagine how this person's feelings are similar to yours?

- **Outside:** Notice that as you brought up these three different feelings, how you looked on the outside might not have changed at all. You could be feeling lonely, afraid, or insecure and still look like you're coping just fine.

It's a good idea to use inside vision any time you hear your mind telling stories about another person, like *She's 100 percent mean.* Instead of treating that story as the absolute truth, try to remain open and curious. Then use your observing skills to try to understand how the other person might be feeling. This will put you in a good position to take effective action to improve the relationship.

Using Inside-Outside Vision

We do have one warning about inside vision: It isn't always accurate. When you try to step into another person's shoes to figure out what that person feels on the inside, there's no way to be 100 percent sure unless you ask—and even then the other person might not tell you or might not tell you the truth. Still, even with this limitation, inside vision is useful. If you never use inside vision, you'll never consider what other people might be thinking or how they're feeling.

Inside-outside vision is a tool. You should use it and not let it use you. For example, inside vision might be using you if you find yourself frequently worrying about what others think: *Does he hate me? Did I do something wrong? Why won't she talk to me?* Remember how we talked about the mind as a problem-finding and problem-solving machine in chapter 7? Also recall that your mind doesn't have all the answers. If it gets stuck worrying about what other people think, that would be a good time to "never mind your mind" and put some of your other BOLD skills to work. Like we've said, relationships are complicated. The best way to build strong relationships is to use a wide variety of tools.

Exercise: Putting Inside-Outside Vision Together with BOLD Skills

A lot of times, your best bet might be to use inside-outside vision together with other BOLD skills. This can be super-helpful when you're having a tough time in friendships. Because inside-outside vision is a way of observing, here's a way you can put it together with other BOLD skills:

1. **Breathe deeply and slow down.** This will help you anchor yourself in the present moment.

2. **Observe.** Use inside-outside vision:

   a. What do you feel on the inside? What do you look like from the outside? For example, do you look cool, angry, insecure, or something else?

   b. How do you think the other person is feeling on the inside? Ask yourself, *If I were that person, how would I feel?* Also notice how the other person looks on the outside.

3. **Listen to your values.** It can be helpful to say something to yourself like *In this situation, I want to be _____* (understanding, forgiving, assertive, and so on).

4. **Decide on actions and do them.** Generate at least four possible responses to the situation and then choose the best one.

Because it can be tough to remember and use all of the steps in real life, especially in difficult situations, this exercise gives you a chance to practice with an imagined situation. Start by thinking about the last big fight or argument you had with someone at school or at home. Imagine the situation vividly. Now let's go through the four BOLD steps.

1. Breathe deeply and slow down.

Think about the fight and breathe in any feelings you were having. Allow those feelings just to be in you. There is plenty of room inside you for all of your feelings.

2. Observe.

Put inside-outside vision to work for you by answering the following questions about the fight.

	You	The other person
Inside vision	How did I think and feel?	If I were the other person, how would I feel?
Outside vision	How did I look on the outside?	How did the other person look on the outside?

3. Listen to your values.

Your values can give you the strength to withstand difficulties and can also point the way to how to respond. Think about what you really care about in the situation you're imagining. Maybe you care about salvaging your relationship with the other person. Maybe you care about standing up for yourself. Maybe there's a way to do both. For example, you could say, "I choose to improve this relationship and be assertive." How do you want to behave in this situation? Do you want to be assertive, honest, friendly, accepting, encouraging, or something else?

4. Decide on actions and do them.

Knowing your values is one thing; acting on them is another, and when you're upset it can be pretty tough to do. Just remember this: Even in a difficult situation, you can choose your actions. You can't choose other people's behavior, but you can choose to respond to them in a way that reflects your values.

Think about the situation you're imagining and try to come up with at least four different ways you could have responded:

1. _____

2. _____

3. _____

4. _____

5. _____

6. _____

Once you've decided on possible actions, you can choose one to *do*. Whatever response you choose, make sure that it's consistent with your values—and that it's likely to make your life easier, or at least not worse. Don't choose strategies that involve withdrawing from your life or getting back at others (unless you value hiding or hurting others).

Wrap-Up

We humans seem to have a lot of trouble getting along. So if you sometimes find it hard to get along with others, congratulations! You're normal.

The good news is that you can use your mindful warrior skills to help improve your relationships. Using inside-outside vision will give you a chance to gain a better understanding of how others might be feeling. And when you put inside-outside vision together with BOLD skills, you can handle even difficult situations. So when things get tough, take the time to breathe deeply and slow down, then observe using inside-outside vision. Listen to your values and let them guide you in deciding on and committing to actions that let you stand for what's important to you. Remember that it's crucial to generate many possible responses to difficult situations. The more you generate, the easier it will be to choose an action that reflects your values.

Chapter 13

seeking your way in the world

BOLD Warrior Skills	
Breathing deeply and slowing down	
Observing	
Listening to your values	✓
Deciding on actions and doing them	✓

Fall seven times, stand up eight.

—Japanese proverb

Chapter 11 focused on your values in regard to yourself, and chapter 12 focused on your values in friendships. In this chapter we'll help you discover your values in regard to how you interact with the wider world around you. You may have heard the saying "Be the change you want to see in the world." That's sort of what this chapter is about. It will help you clarify your values in regard to the world at large. It will also help you chart a path toward achieving your dreams. This kind of success is about being true to your values, being persistent in your efforts, and believing in yourself.

Exercise: Clarifying Your Values in the Wider World

Take a look at the list below, which shows some of the values that people often say are important in areas of life like education, work, or activism. These might sound like big issues, but just as in previous chapters, it's a process of discovery. All you need is the willingness to think, dream, and plan, along with your mindful warrior skills.

Using the same scale of 0 to 10, where 0 is not at all important and 10 is of the greatest impor-tance, rate how important each of these values is to you right now. We've included a few blank spaces where you can fill in any other values that are especially important to you.

0	1	2	3	4	5	6	7	8	9	10
Not important					Moderately important					Of the greatest importance

Importance	Value	Importance	Value
	Building things		Helping others
	Working cooperatively		Persisting
	Promoting fairness		Achieving
	Improving the world		Leading
	Being careful		Keeping promises
	Designing things		Organizing

Once you've rated all of these potential values, take some time to think about the three that you gave the highest ratings. In other words, if you were deciding on and doing actions based on those values, what would you be doing? For example, if achieving is one of your top three values, you might write something like "Achieving in sports is important to me. I want to practice tennis regularly, improve, play fair, and enjoy the sport." As always, remember that values are about what's truly important to you, not what you think is "right" or what you think others would want you to value.

In the space below, describe what it would look like to be acting on those top three values in your life right now.

1. _____

_____

2. _____

_____

3. _____

_____

Exercise: Succeeding on Your Terms

If you're like most people, you feel a lot of pressure to succeed. People or society may have told you that winning is everything. And it often seems that success is measured by getting good outcomes. For example, people may have asked you, "Did you get good grades?" "Did you get chosen for the team?" "Did you get the part in the school play?" "Did you win?"

But are winning and success the same? To help sort this out, read through the following scenarios and then circle the answer that seems right to you.

Scenario 1

Your goal was to get the best grade in science class. You studied hard and even did special projects for extra credit. You got a pretty good grade, but you didn't get the best grade. Did you fail?

Yes   No

Why did you give that answer?

_____

_____

_____

Scenario 2

You value working cooperatively. You did your best to work with a group of classmates on a project, but in the end it fell apart because some of the others didn't do their part. Did you fail?

Yes   No

Why did you give that answer?

_____

_____

_____

Scenario 3

You value promoting fairness. You saw a boy getting bullied and wanted to help him. But when you tried to talk to him about what was going on, he wouldn't say anything. He keeps getting bullied. Did you fail?

Yes   No

Why did you give that answer?

_____

_____

_____

Scenario 4

You want to make the track team. You read all about training, ask for advice from the coach, and really push yourself in your workouts. But when you try out, you don't make the team. Did you fail?

Yes   No

Why did you give that answer?

_____

_____

_____

You may be surprised, but we think that in all four scenarios, you succeeded. Why? Because there are two different types of success—outward and inner—and inner success means living by your values, which is what really counts. Outward success, measured by how well you do in the outside world, is obviously also important, and there's nothing wrong with it.

The big problem with focusing on outward success is that you simply don't have control over everything. You can't control the grades other people get, and you may not even be able to completely control what grades you get. You can't control whether others pull their weight on a group project or how well everyone works together. You can't control whether other people will accept your help. And no matter how much you train, you can't control whether others are stronger or fitter than you. So if you get overly focused on outward success, there's a lot that isn't in your control, and you can become quite miserable when things don't go your way.

You have a lot more control over inner success. Even if you don't get the top grade in science class, you can feel rewarded that you worked hard at learning because you value learning. Even if others don't pull their weight on a group project, you can feel satisfied that you promoted working together. You can feel good about trying to help someone who was getting bullied, and you can get extremely fit even if you don't make the track team. In all of those cases, you'll also have the satisfaction of knowing you behaved consistently with what you care about: your values. You made a sincere effort to do what mattered to you. Sure, the world didn't give you exactly what you wanted. But you still succeeded because you acted in a way that was true to yourself.

Two Principles for Success

Think of some of the most successful people you've heard about—people who are really living their dreams. They might be musicians, athletes, artists, or leaders. What do they have in common? What allowed them to succeed? Did they succeed because of talent, or did they succeed because of hard work?

If you said "talent," you're not alone. Many people think that success comes down to talent, which is generally something you're born with. Ready for a big surprise? If you believe that success comes down to talent, you're actually less likely to succeed—that's right, *less* likely to succeed. This is because people who believe talent is crucial typically don't work as hard as people who believe hard work is crucial.

In fact, talent may be overrated. Top performers look talented because they seem to do things so easily. Think of an Olympic figure skater: She jumps high into the air, does a triple spin, and then lands gracefully on the thin metal blades of her skates. And she makes it seem effortless. As you watch, you probably think, *I could never do that.* However, what you don't see are the countless hours she practiced and the thousands of times she fell down. This brings us to the first principle for success: Succeeding is less about talent and more about practicing.

Principle 1: Top Performers Practice a Lot

Top performers practice a lot more than other people. For example, great violinists practice thousands of hours more than violinists who are merely "good" or "average." There don't seem to be any shortcuts to this kind of achievement. Whether you want to succeed in music, science, painting, sports, writing, or chess, you've got to work hard and dedicate yourself to practicing.

But is practice enough? As it turns out, practice alone won't get you to the top. You have to practice in a particular way. You have to push your limits and be willing to experience difficulty and even distress sometimes.

This brings us to our next point: Sometimes you need to be willing to operate outside your comfort zone.

Principle 2: Top Performers Practice outside Their Comfort Zone

Successful people push themselves and do things that feel really hard at first—maybe even too hard. For example, a world-class figure skater must try jumps that she initially can't do at all. She may fall a hundred times before just barely landing a certain jump. An author could send short stories to dozens of publications—and get dozens of rejection letters—before finally getting something published. An actor risks embarrassment each time he steps onto the stage and improves by taking on a broad range of roles. A master chef needs to concoct new recipes, and some of them may taste terrible.

The truth is, this principle applies to everyone, teenagers included. You have to spend time outside your comfort zone in order to learn new things, expand your skills, and live your dreams. Consider a teenager who's initially way too weak to get on the rowing team but trains twice as hard and eventually gets a place on the team. Another example would be a student who finds English class really hard, but instead of being content with bad grades, keeps sitting at the front of the class, writing and rewriting the assigned essays, and asking for help from the teacher. Or consider a teenager who's super-shy and awkward but keeps going to social events even though it would be easier to stay home. Each of these teenagers is more likely to succeed than someone who gives up.

And what about you? What do you dream of doing in the larger world, and how would practicing hard, outside your comfort zone, change things for you?

Exercise: Going outside Your Comfort Zone

This exercise will help you come up with a plan for succeeding by practicing outside of your comfort zone. Look back at the three values you identified as most important to you at the beginning of this chapter, or choose a new value if you like. Think about how it would look if you were living that value. Choose something you want to improve at and write about it in the space below. For example, "I value achievement and want to become the best piano player I can be" or "I value helping others and want to do something for the homeless."

Write your value here:

_____

_____

Now think about how you can extend yourself beyond your comfort zone by setting a goal that helps you live by your value. For example, you might be willing to take on a challenging piece of music even though it might take months to master, or you might volunteer in a soup kitchen even though you think it will be hard to work with homeless people.

In the space below, describe how you might extend yourself beyond your comfort zone by setting a goal that helps you live your value:

_____

_____

_____

_____

How to Keep Going Even When You Feel Unmotivated

Achieving big dreams usually takes a long time and a lot of hard work. How can you keep feeling inspired and motivated? The short answer is: you can't. As discussed in chapters 5 and 6, it's hard, if not impossible, to control your feelings. Just like you usually can't get rid of difficult emotions, you can't necessarily create positive emotions on demand. There will be times when you just can't make yourself feel inspired.

The good news is that you don't have to *feel* motivated in order to *act* motivated. Here's an example from Sam that illustrates what we mean.

• *Sam: Feeling Stupid and Still Acting on Values*

I cannot believe how stupid I feel. If anyone sees me, I'm going to be laughed out of the neighborhood. Here I am at the local artists' market selling stupid stuff: toilet paper covers. Oh, man, could it get any worse?

The deal is, my grandmother likes to knit these totally bizarre, ugly things: dolls that you put on top of the spare roll of toilet paper in your bathroom. They're incredibly lame, but Gran sells them at the market and then sends the money to poor kids somewhere—I think maybe in Africa. I wish she'd just send them the dolls. Then I wouldn't have to look at them.

Anyway, she asked me if I would help her at her table at the market. She said she's getting a bit tired in her old age and needs somebody to give her a break a few times during the day. I really, really wanted to say no because I figured I'd feel like such a loser standing in front of those toilet paper covers. I wanted to make up an excuse why I couldn't do it, but then I thought about what I care about and what my relationship with Gran means to me. Gran has always been one of my favorite old people. When I was little she used to make cookies just for me, and she always made my favorite kind: chocolate chip. We used to always watch travel shows on TV together, and sometimes we'd come up with plans for trying to end starvation. I loved spending time with her when I was a kid.

So now here I am selling stuff that only a loser would buy. I don't know what I'll do if anyone I know sees me. And if that hot girl Sandy sees me, I will absolutely feel like crawling under the table and dying. But here I am, doing it anyway because I really love Gran and I also think it's pretty cool to want to make a difference for poor kids. One day I might like to find a way to make a difference too. But for now, I'll help Gran with what she's doing, even though it's embarrassing.

Exercise: Coming Up with Sales Tactics for Selling Toilet Paper Covers

Would you feel motivated to sell toilet paper covers at a local artists' market, where anyone in town might see you? Most teens—and probably most adults—would say no. It's kind of a weird thing to sell, and it's definitely not cool. After all, who really needs a cover for the spare roll of toilet paper in the bathroom?

For the purposes of this exercise, let's assume that you feel totally uninspired about selling these dolls. The question is, could you still stand behind that table selling them even if you didn't feel motivated? Could you even go so far as to think up some creative ways to promote them? Take a minute now to step outside your comfort zone and think up some strategies for helping sell the dolls.

Write your ideas in the space below. Be sure to write at least a couple of ideas, no matter how weird or crazy they seem:

_____

_____

_____

_____

_____

Did you come up with some ideas? If so, that's great! If not, try again and really give it your best shot. Imagine your life depends on it. Be sure you've written something before you read on.

So what's the point of this exercise—to help Sam or to help you launch a successful career in marketing weird, embarrassing objects? Hardly. The point is, even if you don't feel motivated to promote those toilet paper covers, you can still decide to take actions in support of that goal. Think about it: even though you couldn't care less about toilet paper covers, just like Sam you found a way to act as if you care.

If you can do that for something you don't care about, what about all of the things you *do* care about—the things you want to do in this world? Do you sometimes feel unmotivated to do them? That's perfectly normal. Everyone feels that way at times. Novelists often don't feel like writing, yet those who are successful write every day, even when they don't feel inspired. Top athletes work out even when they don't feel like it. Successful students keep studying even when they feel bored. In summary, it's valuable to remember the following two points:

- Difficult feelings and thoughts don't have to stop you from doing what you care about.

- Lack of feeling (for example, lack of motivation or inspiration) doesn't have to stop you either.

Steps to Success in Living Your Dreams

Values don't mean a lot until you act on them. Yet sometimes it's hard. Maybe you feel embarrassed, like Sam. Maybe you feel scared about trying something new or difficult. Or maybe you sometimes lack motivation or inspiration. As you now know, none of those things have to stand in your way. Still, what specifically can you do to increase your chances of living your dreams? Here are some recommendations, illustrated by examples from Sam's situation.

1. **Set goals that are specific.** Be clear about exactly what you plan to do and when. For example, Sam decided to help his grandmother sell her dolls at the market on a specific day.

2. **When you feel yourself resisting, remind yourself why you're taking specific actions.** Remind yourself how a certain action or goal furthers your values. For example, Sam was motivated by his love for his grandmother, his desire to help her, and a wish to someday follow her example and find ways to help others.

3. **Think of the benefits of achieving your goals.** How will your actions further your values? How will they benefit you or others? For example, Sam described some warm feelings about helping his grandmother and some satisfaction about helping kids in need. Ultimately, those things were more important to Sam than feeling embarrassed.

4. **Be real!** Plan for difficulties. Setting and achieving goals can bring up a lot of challenges. It's important that you be honest with yourself and anticipate any obstacles that might make achieving the goal tough. A quick way to plan for obstacles is by using if-then statements: "If _____ (describe the difficulty), then I will _____ (describe how you'll overcome it)." For example, Sam recognized that he'd feel stupid and embarrassed and that he might try to get out of selling the toilet paper covers. So he came up with

an if-then statement about this: "If I end up feeling stupid, then I'll remind myself why the goal is important and keep putting my best effort into selling those dolls."

The Wrap-Up

Top performers usually make things look easy, but this is because of all the hours and work they've put into developing their skills—and because they've been willing to operate outside their comfort zone. It's likely that they experienced many failures along the way. But ultimately they succeeded because they persisted with what they cared about.

To live your dreams, you'll have to accept the inevitable failures along the way. Be prepared! Failure brings up a lot of emotional pain. Use the approaches in chapters 5 and 6 to help you be willing to have difficult feelings as you keep moving toward the things you care about.

Failures will also make you doubt yourself. Use the approaches in chapters 7 through 9 to observe when your mind is criticizing you and then practice observing those thoughts and watching them come and go, just like bad weather comes and goes. You don't have to fight it.

Sometimes you won't live by your values. Sometimes you won't achieve your goals. Sometimes you won't try as hard as you could have. Sometimes you won't try at all. The key question isn't whether you'll wander off your valued path. Of course you will. Everyone does.

The key question is whether you'll return to your valued path. When you fail, will you persist and keep turning back in the direction of your values? If your answer is yes, before you know it you'll find that you're traveling in the direction of your values—and that makes life an amazing journey.

Conclusion

the spark you carry
in your heart

Youth is, after all, just a moment, but it is the moment, the spark, that you always carry in your heart.

—Raisa Gorbachev

At the beginning of this book, we said that we wrote it for *you*, not for anyone who may have asked you to read it. Now we want to honor that statement by giving you the chance to write your own ending—a personalized description of your journey through the book, what you've learned, what the concepts mean to you in your life, and what messages you'll take with you as you continue your journey in life.

"Journey in life" may sound like something huge—maybe something frightening. But it's actually something you've always been doing. You proceed on this journey every day when you wake up, get dressed, and go about your day. However, there is a difference between the journey you've been on and the one you'll describe here. Now you have a better understanding that this journey is about you and your values, and you know that, ultimately, the choice of what you do and how you do it is up to you.

Through the course of this book, you've learned that everyone has difficult thoughts and feelings but those thoughts and feelings come and go, just like the weather. And you also understand that while the human mind is wonderful beyond measure and capable of amazing inventions, it can also be a troublemaker. One thing we can't do with the mind is make it stop or force it to think the thoughts we want. We will inevitably experience the mind's many roles: problem finder, storyteller, and evaluator.

You've also learned that feelings are both powerful and natural. There are (and always will be) times when you wish you were free of sadness and insecurity. Yet these feelings are connected to what's important to you. Sadness often indicates that you've lost something you love. Insecurity often indicates that you really want to succeed or excel at something. As long as you love and dream, sometimes you'll feel sadness and insecurity.

The key is having the courage to make space for your feelings and the wisdom to pursue what you care about even when you hear your mind say you can't do it. You've learned BOLD warrior skills that will allow you to make space for your feelings and "never mind your mind," and this will help you act even when you doubt yourself. Now you just need to practice those skills. To send you on your unique journey, here's one final exercise. It will help you put all of the pieces in the book together in a way that reflects you and your values.

Exercise: Connecting the Pieces

The following pages have a graphic with puzzle pieces, many of them representing the main ideas in this book. Take some time to use this graphic as a foundation for expressing what you learned from this book. You can do it in any way that you like: drawing, writing, or whatever. Just be creative. As you depict your story, notice how all the different parts of you interconnect. That is wise view indeed!

Jess and Sam have started to work on this graphic to describe their journeys and the things they have learned. Take a look at their samples and see how the pieces fit together for them.

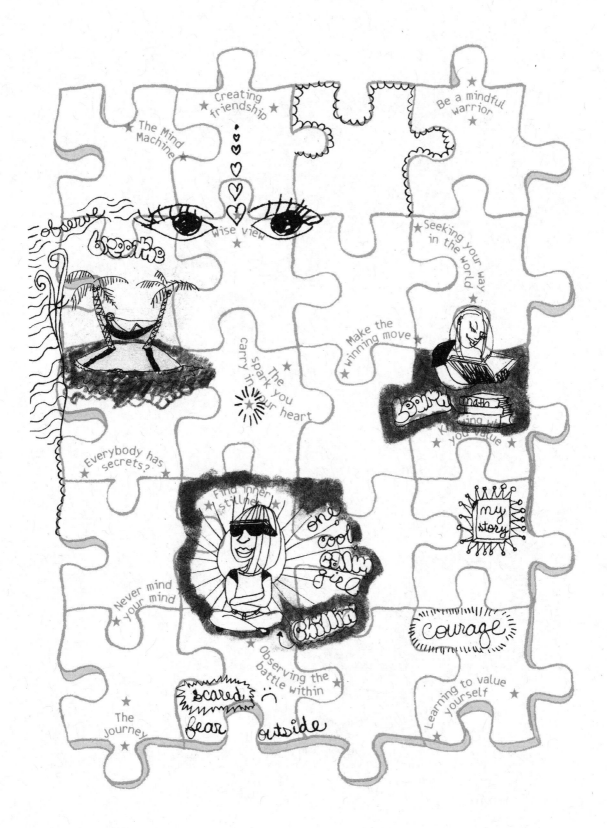

resources

This book is linked to a website that provides resources for teenagers, parents, and educators. Go to www.actforadolescents.com for more resources. If you're a teenager, the place to check out more resources is mindfulwarriors.com.

Professional Training and Workshops

Louise Hayes and Joseph Ciarrochi conduct training workshops around the world for professionals working with adolescents. For more information on Joseph and Ann Bailey, go to acceptandchange.com, and for more information on Louise Hayes, go to www.louisehayes.com.au.

ACT Textbooks and Self-Help Books

A wide range of books and self-help books based in acceptance and commitment therapy (ACT; the approach used in this book) are available from New Harbinger. For further information go to newharbinger.com.

The Association for Contextual Behavioral Science

For more information on ACT, a good resource is the Association for Contextual Behavioral Science, a worldwide online learning and research community dedicated to the advancement of cognitive and behavioral science and practice to alleviate human suffering and advance well-being. For more information go to contextualpsychology.org. Information on ACT for the general public is also available at this website if you click on the ACT link. There you will find general information as well as lists of therapists and coaches and other resources, including reading material, e-mail discussion groups, and podcasts.

references

Hayes, S. C., K. D. Strosahl, and K. G. Wilson. 1999. *Acceptance and Commitment Therapy: An Experiential Approach to Behavior Change.* New York: Guilford Press.

Neff, K., and P. McGehee. 2010. "Self-Compassion and Psychological Resilience among Adolescents and Young Adults." *Self and Identity* 9(3):225–40.

Syed, M. 2010. *Bounce: Mozart, Federer, Picasso, Beckham, and the Science of Success.* New York: HarperCollins.

Wilson, K. G., with T. DuFrene. (2009). *Mindfulness for Two: An Acceptance and Commitment Therapy Approach to Mindfulness in Psychotherapy.* Oakland, CA: New Harbinger Publications.

Joseph V. Ciarrochi, PhD, is professor of psychology at the University of Western Sydney and an active researcher with numerous national competitive grants. His research focuses on understanding and developing social and emotional well-being. Ciarrochi has written over eighty international journal articles, books, and book chapters, and is regularly invited to speak at conferences and leading universities and institutions around the world. He has authored and edited eight books related to the promotion of mental health and well-being.

Louise Hayes, PhD, is a clinical psychologist and academic with the University of Melbourne in Australia. She has devoted her career to helping young people and their families. She is a leader in adapting acceptance and commitment therapy (ACT) for adolescents, researches the outcomes of ACT for young people, and conducts ACT training for professionals internationally.

Ann Bailey, MA, is an experienced clinical practitioner who helps people manage their emotions and live more vital lives.

Foreword writer **Steven C. Hayes, PhD,** is Foundation Professor of Psychology at the University of Nevada, Reno. He is the author of innumerable books and scientific articles, including the successful ACT workbook *Get Out of Your Mind and Into Your Life.*

More ⏱ Instant Help Books for Teens

A Division of New Harbinger Publications, Inc.

THE ANXIETY WORKBOOK FOR TEENS
Activities to Help You Deal with Anxiety & Worry
ISBN: 978-1572246034 / US $14.95
Also available as an e-book at newharbinger.com

THE STRESS REDUCTION WORKBOOK FOR TEENS
Mindfulness Skills to Help You Deal with Stress
ISBN: 978-1572246973 / US $15.95
Also available as an e-book at newharbinger.com

THINK CONFIDENT, BE CONFIDENT FOR TEENS
A Cognitive Therapy Guide to Overcoming Self-Doubt & Creating Unshakable Self-Esteem
ISBN: 978-1608821136 / US $16.95
Also available as an e-book at newharbinger.com

COPING WITH CLIQUES
A Workbook to Help Girls Deal with Gossip, Put-Downs, Bullying & Other Mean Behavior
ISBN: 978-1572246133 / US $16.95
Also available as an e-book at newharbinger.com

DON'T LET YOUR EMOTIONS RUN YOUR LIFE FOR TEENS
Dialectical Behavior Therapy Skills for Helping You Manage Mood Swings, Control Angry Outbursts & Get Along with Others
ISBN: 978-1572248830 / US $16.95
Also available as an e-book at newharbinger.com

BEYOND THE BLUES
A Workbook to Help Teens Overcome Depression
ISBN: 978-1572246119 / US $14.95
Also available as an e-book at newharbinger.com

new harbingerpublications, inc.
1-800-748-6273 / newharbinger.com

Like us on Facebook

Follow us on Twitter
@newharbinger.com

(VISA, MC, AMEX / prices subject to change without notice)

Don't miss out on new books in the subjects that interest you.
Sign up for our **Book Alerts** at **newharbinger.com**

ARE YOU SEEKING A CBT THERAPIST?
The Association for Behavioral & Cognitive Therapies (ABCT) Find-a-Therapist service offers a list of therapists schooled in CBT techniques. Therapists listed are licensed professionals who have met the membership requirements of ABCT & who have chosen to appear in the directory.
Please visit www.abct.org & click on *Find a Therapist*.